HOW TO DEVELOP
YOUR SIXTH SENSE

A practical guide to developing
your own extraordinary powers

DAVID LAWSON

Thorsons

THIS BOOK IS DEDICATED TO EVERYONE WHO
HAS EVER TRUSTED ME WITH THEIR PSYCHIC
SECRETS. IN THIS WAY I HAVE LEARNED MUCH
ABOUT THE INNATE PSYCHIC ABILITY WITHIN
US ALL AND RECEIVED CONFIRMATION OF MY
OWN GROWING PSYCHIC AWARENESS.
WITH LOVE, DAVID

Thorsons
An Imprint of HarperCollins*Publishers*
77–85 Fulham Palace Road,
Hammersmith, London w6 8jb

The Thorsons website address is: www.thorsons.com

First published by Thorsons as *Principles of Your Psychic Potential* 1997
This edition published by Thorsons 2001

9   10

© David Lawson 1997

David Lawson asserts the moral right to
be identified as the author of this work

A catalogue record for this book
is available from the British Library

ISBN 0 00 711700 0

Printed and bound in Great Britain by
Martins the Printers Limited, Berwick upon Tweed

ABOUT THE AUTHOR:

David Lawson is an English healer, writer and course leader. Together with partner Justin Carson he travels the world teaching self-healing techniques, hands-on healing, psychic development and spiritual growth.

His books include *Star Healing – Your Sun Sign, Your Health and Your Success* (Hodder & Stoughton), *Money and Your Life – A Prosperity Playbook* (with Justin Carson; Healing Workshops Press), *So You Want to be a Shaman* (Godsfield Press), *A Company of Angels* and *You Can Channel!* (Findhorn Press) and, for Thorsons, *I See Myself in Perfect Health – Your Essential Guide to Self-healing* and *Principles of Self-healing* (Thorsons). He is perhaps best known for his book and divination pack based upon the gods and goddesses of the Egyptians, *The Eye of Horus – An Oracle of Ancient Egypt* (UK: Piatkus Books; US: St. Martin's Press; Australia: Simon and Schuster).

David's work has been featured in numerous magazine articles, radio shows and television programmes. Most recently he has been a regular contributor to a popular daytime show on Sky Television. His audio tapes include the guided visualizations *I See Myself in Perfect Health* volumes I & II and the *Money and Your Life Prosperity Course*, all produced by Healing Workshops Press.

David and Justin are authorized world-wide facilitators of courses based on *You Can Heal Your Life* by Louise L. Hay. For details of these and other forthcoming events based upon their own material please write to:

Healing Workshops
PO Box 1678
London NW5 4EW
UK

ACKNOWLEDGEMENTS

I would like to thank the following people for their help in the writing and publication of this book:

Susan Mears, Michelle Pilley, Michele Turney, Caroline Tomlin, Hattie Madden, Barbara Vesey, Paul Redhead, Jo Ridgeway, Michael Spender, Louise McNamara, Helen Elwes, Amanda McKelvie, Lilian and Eric Lawson, Anne and Alex Carson, Star (Maggie Whiteley), Stephanie Holland, David Morton, Barbara A. King, Jo Neary, the delicious Kitty Campion and all of my friends, family, clients and guides.

Special thanks to Louise L. Hay for her inspiration and encouragement, and also to my partner Justin Carson whose practical support, ideas, good humour and care make it possible for me to write.

David Lawson
London, March 1997

CONTENTS

chapter one

OPENING THE DOORS

YOUR PSYCHIC POTENTIAL

We all have our own unique psychic potential. We have abilities
– to see, hear, feel and know – which go beyond the range of our
purely physical senses of sight, hearing, touch, taste and smell.
We are able to receive, access and transmit vast quantities of
information, and we can learn to strengthen these abilities.
Would you be surprised to hear that our intuitive and psychic
senses are just as natural and normal as any of our five physical
ones? Perhaps this information is new for you, or perhaps you
have always instinctively felt that you have greater intuitive and
sensory resources than you have yet learned to access and make
use of?

For some, reading this book will be a voyage of discovery into
areas that may initially seem quite familiar to you. The rich
landscape of images, ideas, exercises and techniques that I offer
you in the pages that follow will serve to remind you, first and
foremost, of what you already know and are actively able to do.
With practice they will introduce you to an even wider range of
abilities and help you to tap into greater depth, colour, substance

and sensation. Whether you are taking your first steps towards psychic knowledge or learning how to run towards it, filled with the excitement of having constantly expanding areas of intuitive awareness, please remember that psychic potential is latent within us all, just waiting to be discovered. It is your psychic potential that has guided you to this book, and it will continue to guide you as you develop.

WE ARE ALL PSYCHIC!

Many of us are already using our psychic abilities without even knowing that we are doing it, and many more are aware of the information that they receive through their 'inner' senses but do not talk about it – often for fear that other people will not understand. Psychic potential is not something that some people have and others not; we may just be more awake to our abilities or more naturally developed in some areas than many other people we know. However, each of our friends, colleagues and family members has her or his own unique range of psychic senses too, some awake and some dormant, just waiting to be discovered. Perhaps it is we who are just waking up? Whatever is true for you, be assured that the potential is there within you and that your potential is also special and unique.

Do you sometimes think of someone two minutes before they telephone you? Do you walk into a room and pick up an atmosphere within a couple of seconds? Do you receive strong mental images or hear the answer to a question that you have inside your head before you have voiced it? Can you feel when others are upset or excited even before they speak to you or before you look in their direction to pick up the usual, physical signals? Do you have a sense that you could be able to give healing, or send thoughts to others that they will hear inside their mind? If the answer to any of these is 'yes' or even 'perhaps', this could be an indication of your unique psychic potential.

This book is concerned with awakening your psychic potential and helping you to utilize your psychic abilities for your personal development, spiritual growth, self-healing and success. In doing so, you may discover that you have abilities which you could use to help other people and support them with their development, too.

MY PSYCHIC ABILITIES

My own psychic abilities are chiefly concerned with healing, although I have a range of clairvoyant, clairaudient, clairsentient and channelling abilities that support me in this. Since childhood I have had an intuitive awareness of the mental, emotional and spiritual factors that contribute to disease, disharmony, relationship difficulties and a number of other personal challenges which many of us face. Perhaps more importantly, I have also been blessed with an ability to help other people to find their own solutions to these challenges; helping them to stimulate their awareness, become attuned to their underlying spiritual purpose and grow into their personal power. For this reason, the psychic awakening I teach others to do for themselves is always concerned with healing, first and foremost.

This is not a book full of information about seeing ghoulish apparitions, holding seances, indulging in psychic espionage or being able to do supernatural party pieces. To be more precise, it does not reflect the view of psychic abilities that we may have received through the mass media. Television, particularly, has a tendency to entertain by being as thrilling, shocking or controversial as it can be whenever the subject of psychic awareness is 'in the frame'. Fortunately this has improved in recent years as more people working behind and in front of the cameras have developed a healthier view of psychic phenomena. However, like me, you may have grown up with pantomime horror movies that were filled with images of clanking chains, seances that have gone terribly wrong or 'spooky' people who can look into our minds. If this has left you with any fear of developing your own psychic potential, then let that go now. What we are about to explore is completely safe and, if you choose to continue the exploration, is ultimately much more valuable and entertaining.

This is a book about spiritual evolution and positive personal development. The doors that I will help you to open can also help you on your path to greater joy, fulfilment and success, enabling you to become more aligned to your higher awareness and enhancing your essential nature. If you have an ability to see or hear people in spirit or are able to intuit what other people are thinking or feeling, then there is plenty that will support your abilities here.

Let us begin by discussing some of the main areas of psychic ability. As you read through the descriptions of these sensory areas, notice if your instincts draw you to one or two in particular. Do you already have abilities in these areas or do you have a hunch that you may be able to develop them? Read on!

CLAIRVOYANCE

Clairvoyance literally means 'clear sight'. A person with developed clairvoyant abilities has a strong sense of inner vision, and is able to receive information in the form of visual images or symbols. Most clairvoyants receive their information internally: some describe having something akin to a cinema screen inside their head with images moving across it; others receive individual symbols that they learn to interpret. Some clairvoyants receive information externally: they are able to see people or animals in spirit, or can observe the subtle energy that circulates around themselves when they walk into a room.

Clairvoyance is a term that is often incorrectly used to apply to a wider range of psychic abilities than just the visual ability to perceive and receive information. Indeed, the language of psychic abilities is very visually-orientated. We talk about someone being able to 'look' into the future, and describe a person with this gift as being a 'visionary' or a 'seer'. Perhaps this is indicative of the many people who have a natural aptitude for developing clear sight, or perhaps it indicates that many more people who are skilled in some other area also have a degree of developed clairvoyance.

AURIC SIGHT

Auric sight is easily linked with clairvoyance because it is an ability that also relies upon a visual sense. However, while many clairvoyants may have, in addition, a developed sense of auric sight, there are many differences between the two skills, not least in regard to the nature of the information received.

The *aura* is a subtle energetic emanation that surrounds all living things and, as surprising as this may seem to some, surrounds all inanimate objects too. To explain it as simply as possible, it is often described as being like a subtle electrical or magnetic energy that radiates from human beings, animals, plants, stones, machinery, buildings, household objects and anything else that you can think of. Even your favourite sofa or armchair has an aura.

Most of us feel auras even if we do not see them. It is quite common these days to talk about a person having a particularly positive aura. Aside from all of the physical information that we receive about a person's appearance, body language and voice tone, the information that we receive from someone's aura has a profound effect on how we feel about that person when we first meet. Some people are considered to be particularly charismatic or compelling. This is often because their aura is bright, attractive and engaging.

A person with auric sight will not only feel these subtle emanations but will also be able to see them. For some, the auric field will appear as a very subtle movement of energy or light around a person or object of focus. This can be a bit like a double or 'ghost' image around figures on a television set when it is not correctly tuned in to the signal. Others will see auras in this way but will also see some subtle colouration within that energy, commonly a silvery blue or grey. People with the most developed auric sight will see a full range of bright, vivid colours. Although as a child I had always seen subtle energetic fields around me, I was initially startled when, at 17, I first started to see colours in this way. Whilst alone and meditating I suddenly found that I could see colours around everything: my hands, my body, the mirror on the wall and even the bed that I was sitting upon. It was as if someone had flicked a switch and everything was bathed or surrounded with colour.

Most people who are willing to practise are able to develop some degree of auric sight, and there are many positive uses for this kind of information. If you have already experienced any of the phenomena that I have described above, you may have a strong, natural ability to see in this way.

CLAIRAUDIENCE

Clairaudience is the term used for psychic hearing abilities. It can be literally defined as 'clear hearing'. A clairaudient person receives psychic information in the form of subtle sounds, words or ideas that are perceived and interpreted through the hearing centres of the brain. Some people report that they hear voices which give them direct information about themselves or about the needs, feelings, actions or motivations of other people. Others do not tangibly 'hear' in this way, they just seem to know things as if they had heard about them.

Latent clairaudients often report a range of sensations within or around their ears. Many seem to be able to 'feel' with their ears as well as listen. Some may have such an acute ability to hear that their ears and their temperament become over-sensitive to loud, sharp or persistent noise. Their mood, attitude and health can be easily affected by the sounds that surround them, and they may actively choose to live in a silent or peaceful environment for this reason. Many more will avoid extremely noisy or discordant environments whenever possible.

Many people have a degree of clairaudience but do not recognize it as such because, like so many other psychic abilities, it has always been there. We may have always received words, thoughts or sounds of inspiration inside our mind without ever questioning their source and their precise nature. Numerous 'good ideas' may have originated as clairaudient messages or as information perceived through one of our other psychic senses. We sometimes expect the first stirrings of our psychic potential to be accompanied by fanfares and fireworks, and this can sometimes be the case, but often we are so used to what we can hear, see or sense that we do not particularly notice it.

CLAIRSENTIENCE

Clairsentience is particularly common, especially amongst women and children, who are still generally more emotionally based than men. As children we are all quite open intuitively and emotionally; then, as we grow, we may learn to shut out these aspects of our awareness. Boys and men still receive messages that they have to be logical and dispassionate, and that emotional sensitivity is a bad thing. Male or female, to develop good clairsentience we need to unlearn the judgements and restrictions that were applied to us when we were growing up and become more emotionally and intuitively 'vulnerable'.

Clairsentience is a term used to define the range of senses that are operating when we get a 'gut feeling' about another person or a 'gut reaction' to something that is happening to us. The term 'gut feeling' is a good one because it quite rightly indicates that we often receive the information within our bodies rather than in our minds. While frequently it is the stomach area that we are most aware of in this respect, the chest, heart and solar plexus are also particularly sensitive.

TELEPATHY

Beloved of science fiction and horror writers, telepathy is often associated with stories about psychic spying, brainwashing and manipulation. The reality is quite different, far less sensational but much more satisfying and, on the whole, quite safe. In fact, we are all telepathic to some degree and go about our daily lives transmitting and receiving information without being consciously aware that we are doing so for much of the time. While we each transmit and receive in different ways, the basic principle is the same: we all act like radios which are able to tune in to information and send out our own signals on certain frequencies. Some of us have a greater ability to receive, others are more able to transmit.

Our individual telepathic abilities are closely linked to our other psychic gifts. If we are more clairvoyant than clairaudient, for instance, then we are much more likely to receive our telepathic information in the form of visual images or symbols than to 'hear' the thoughts of other people in our head.

Telepathic clairsentients may receive a sense of another person's physical or emotional state, even at a distance.

Telepathy can operate at short distances and at great ones. We certainly experience short-distance telepathy on a regular basis with our families and close friends. In these cases, our telepathic abilities become entwined with our other abilities to read and transmit information. For instance, we often know when someone we are close to is angry with us, even when she or he does not express it openly. We may pick up a combination of signals that includes body language, tone of voice, changes in behaviour and clairsentient emotional messages as well as telepathic thoughts that the person transmits and we receive, loud and clear. In addition, most of us at some time experience having the same idea as our partner, parent, friend or child at exactly the same moment as she or he has it.

Long-distance telepathy can be just as common as the telepathy we experience at close range, though perhaps it can appear more remarkable because we do not have the more obvious physical signals to rely upon. I regularly think about friends from around the world just as they are writing me a letter or as they are contemplating telephoning me. In fact, even at close range I frequently think about people before they contact me or before I bump into them. Of course, it is not always clear who thought of whom first!

HANDS-ON HEALING

Hands-on healing has been given many names and is taught and practised using a variety of systems world-wide, but the essential nature of this healing art remains the same. Hands-on healing is the ability to channel a range of spiritual, magnetic or vital energies for the purpose of stimulating the innate self-healing abilities of others. Often these energies are transmitted from one person to another via the hands, hence 'hands-on' healing. A healer may physically place her or his hands upon the head or body of the recipient and allow the energy available to flow through him or her and into any area, physical, mental or emotional, that is in need of healing support. However, physical contact is not an essential part of this process, and many healers work by placing their hands near the recipient rather than on her or his body, sending energy through the auric body first, which finds its way to wherever it is needed physically.

Traditionally this kind of healing has often been called spiritual healing or faith healing. The term spiritual healing is relevant because the healing does occur on the spiritual level first and, through the spiritual, is then able to affect changes holistically throughout the entire system. 'Faith healing', although a term that is still commonly applied to these abilities, is inaccurate and greatly misleading. It implies that faith is essential for healing to occur and suggests that these abilities are inextricably linked to religious beliefs. Neither is true; the recipient just needs to be willing to experiment with this kind of healing for it to be of benefit. Many people who have no spiritual or religious beliefs, and who are initially cynical about the efficacy of consulting healers, have benefited greatly from healing treatments. For the healers themselves, there is no need to subscribe to any particular faith or creed in order to develop these abilities successfully.

The exchange of healing energy can be given by people of all ages and from all social, economic, cultural and religious backgrounds. Similarly, everyone can benefit from healing, regardless of condition, background or beliefs. You do not even have to be sick to benefit. Many people who are essentially healthy visit healers on a regular basis to help maintain their health and to enhance the quality of their lives.

Some healers do not even get physically close to the people they are helping, but are instead able to channel healing energy from the other side of a room or even from a great distance. Good counsellors frequently channel healing energy to their clients, often without being consciously aware of what they are doing. Numerous healers engage in distant or absent healing, and it is possible to send healing energy even to someone on the other side of the world.

Everyone can learn to give healing. Some people have a highly developed healing gift, but with practice and a willingness to experiment it is something that we can all do. I have often taught complete beginners to give hands-on healing in under two hours; even if some individuals are unsure of the quality or the validity of what they are doing, the recipients usually report tangible feelings of peace, relaxation and harmony, and derive great benefit from the experience. Of course, as with any other skill, mastery comes with time, patience, persistence and fine tuning.

CHANNELLING

The word 'channel' appears to have come from America and covers a broad spectrum of psychic abilities and creative expression. Any of us can be said to be channelling when we lose ourselves in the creative process of painting a picture, writing a book or at any other time when we let go to our creative muse. Some channelling is similar to old-style mediumship, as the channel could be someone who acts as a vehicle for family or friends wishing to communicate from other realms. However, before you get visions of the comic, eccentric mediums found in old movies, let me give you the wider picture.

Healers channel healing energy, acting as a vehicle for healing light. Psychics can channel guidance or information in the form of mental pictures (clairvoyance), hearing subtle sounds or words (clairaudience) and in many other ways. Channelling can be directly spoken, or written in the form of automatic writing. Channels can pass on information from spirit guides and teachers. Some people also channel a form of their own higher mind or higher wisdom. There is really no mystery; we are all capable of learning to channel positive, inspirational guidance.

THE HIGHER MIND

The terms 'the higher mind' and 'the higher consciousness' are gaining mainstream recognition these days. They refer to the concept that each of us has a part of our consciousness that acts as a bridge between the spiritual and the mental dimensions of our awareness. Simply put, we each have a reservoir of higher thought and wisdom which helps to guide the course of our lives. This part of ourselves is better able to see the bigger picture of the daily events and dramas that we become engrossed in and, if we are willing to listen to it, will enable us to put everything into perspective. Acting with the grace of our higher self can help us to make the life choices that will best support our underlying spiritual purpose and guide us in the direction of our greatest joy and fulfilment. It is highly likely that the best decisions you have ever made began as ideas or impulses that were placed in your conscious awareness by your higher mind.

The process of actively developing your psychic potential will automatically strengthen your connection to your higher mind and allow you to work with it more effectively. The higher mind communicates to us in many ways, including sending messages to us through our psychic and intuitive senses. A certain amount of good psychic work is channelled directly from our higher consciousness which, as well as being a reservoir of wisdom in itself, acts as a bridge for information that is transmitted to us from external sources such as spirit guides and helpers.

SPIRIT GUIDES AND HELPERS

Spirit guides are personalities or energies of support that work with us to assist us in our development and the pursuit of our higher purpose. Some people choose to think of them as another aspect of their own higher mind or greater consciousness, but I tend to agree with the school of thought that considers them to be entities who are completely external to us and who communicate to us through our higher awareness and, potentially, through our psychic senses.

When I began actively to develop my hands-on healing abilities, I received some powerful tuition from a healing guide in spirit who I believe is still around me, keeping an eye on the healing work that I do. Indeed, I have been aware of a number of guiding spirits supporting me as I have worked on individual and group healing, counselling and teaching sessions. The knowledge that I have access to support and guidance in all areas of my life has been greatly comforting to me during the times of personal challenge I have faced, even when I have been too wrapped up in my own personal dramas to remember to ask for help!

Spirit guides can be the source of a considerable amount of psychic information. Our own guides may communicate with us psychically to advise us about our own personal development or to support us with information for someone who is seeking our help and counsel. Other people's guides may choose to communicate through us, so that they can pass on valuable insights to the person with whom they are working.I make a number of references to spirit guides throughout this book, particularly within Chapter 6, when I talk about the direct channelling of information.

THE LINK BETWEEN PHYSICAL AND PSYCHIC SENSES

In my experience there is often a powerful relationship between the physical senses with which we are most comfortable and the psychic senses we can most easily access and develop. For example, if you are a visual person who easily thinks in pictures and whose language is very visually orientated, then it is highly likely that you will be able to receive psychic information visually. A person who always notices what things look like and who, when asked to describe an experience, will tend to talk about its visual elements rather than the sounds, feelings, tastes or smells associated with it, is likely to be attuned to receiving and interpreting information in the form of pictures, symbols or filmic sequences.

Latent clairvoyants may work in jobs that allow them to design, visualize, paint, style or illustrate. They may choose a visual art as a hobby and be particularly affected by the appearance of people, objects or environments. However, this is a guideline, not a rule; there are many people who are highly clairvoyant and who do not consider themselves to be visually inclined. Indeed, people who lose their physical sight have sometimes been known to develop a strong clairvoyant sense as a result of their disability.

People with strong visual skills may also be particularly attuned to developing auric vision, or may learn to channel visual information. In fact, many people work as psychic artists by allowing their technical ability to draw or paint to be the vehicle for translating the visual information that they receive.

If you are a good listener, the kind of person who is particularly skilled at listening intently to what other people have to say, or good at discerning changes of tone, pitch and frequency of noise, then you may well be a latent clairaudient. Auditory people are often drawn to work or create with sound, which could include a range of musical skills, voice work and sound recognition. In addition, they may describe their experiences in terms of the sounds that they heard and whom or what they were listening to. Indeed, for many, loud, sustained, persistent or high-pitched sounds which other people may not even notice will be unbearable.

Clairaudients are often people who think in words or sounds first before converting this information into feelings, pictures or concepts. People who have an affinity with words and sounds are also likely to have a latent ability to act as a channel for direct verbal or written information.

If you respond to life emotionally or in a tactile manner and you are the kind of person whose chief response to life is based upon feelings, then you could easily be a latent clairsentient. You may also be a natural hands-on healer. Many people who are naturally empathic, passionate or compassionate find that they have clairsentient ability, or may be drawn to one of a number of healing arts that allow them to work with their hands and heal through direct physical contact.

Clairsentients often feel things quite intensely. Indeed, clairsentients who have not learned to regulate and protect their sensitivity can be powerfully affected by other people's moods. Similarly, natural healers may gain an impression of another person's physical or emotional state within the sensations of their own body and emotions. Clairsentients and healers are often people who have a strongly developed emotional intelligence but who, in some cases, may not always be able to voice what they are feeling. Sometimes, feelings are too big to be translated into words. However, a good, professional clairsentient or healer will often learn to bridge the gap between gut intuition and intellect.

PREPARING YOURSELF TO BEGIN

There are no absolute requirements for anyone who chooses to embark upon a journey of psychic development. The principles that I offer within this book are meant as guidelines, not hard-and-fast rules. However, it is best to begin with the right intentions. If you are developing psychically from a position of strength, this will be reflected within the success and stability of your development. Therefore, endeavour to take care of your physical well-being at all times.

I would not recommend any psychic development that is linked to the use of recreational or psychedelic drugs. Anything mood-altering or hallucinogenic could potentially open your psychic senses artificially, but this kind of opening is usually damaging, unstable and ultimately limiting. If you open up your awareness naturally then you open up safely and are better able to stabilize and build upon the positive potential of your newfound psychic skills. Ideally it is also best to keep alcohol, nicotine and caffeine consumption to a minimum. While there have been a number of talented psychics who have been chain smokers, mild alcoholics or coffee addicts, the majority of us function better psychically (and otherwise) when the use of these substances is minimal.

For myself, it was the process of developing as a healer and a psychic that prompted me to give up cigarettes and alcohol. It became apparent to me that it was not comfortable for me to continue using these drugs and develop my abilities at the same time, and the latter was a much more attractive and satisfying option. I have never regretted making that choice! Whatever you choose for yourself, maintain an intention to care for yourself physically, emotionally, mentally and spiritually and do your best to practise that intention in whatever way that your instincts tell you is appropriate.

In preparation it is also useful to think about your motives for developing psychically. What is it that you want or need from this process of development? How would you like to develop and what effect would you expect your psychic awareness to have upon other areas of your life? From my experience, people who wish to grow psychically as part of their ongoing spiritual evolution and their progression towards their highest potential are those who are likely to have the most satisfying and rewarding process of awakening. In addition, it often helps to have an intention to help and support the growth or healing of others with our innate abilities, although this is certainly not essential. However, the desire to grow and the desire to serve others often go hand in hand; one stimulates the other.

CREATING THE RIGHT ENVIRONMENT

There are a number of exercises in this book which you might choose to practise with a friend or partner, and working with other people is certainly to be recommended. However, I have written many of these exercises to be primarily performed alone, in a safe, comfortable place where you are unlikely to be disturbed. Find or create a space in your home that feels warm, comfortable and secure and make it as conducive to peace and relaxation as you can. In preparing your environment you might like to follow the guidelines that I offer below. They will prove to be helpful but, once again, they are not essential.

Exercise: Your Sacred Space

Once you have chosen the space that you are going to use to conduct most of your initial psychic development, take some time to cleanse it and personalize it.

1] Physically clear this area of excessive clutter and debris.

2] Spend some time cleansing and brightening the energy of this space by playing beautiful music, burning essential oils, lighting candles, singing, chanting or visualizing this area filled with bright, healing, protective light. Do whatever feels appropriate for you.

Essential oils, the natural oils of flowers and plants, and essential oil burners are readily available these days. Jasmine oil and Rose oil are wonderful for psychic work, but good Jasmine and Rose can be quite expensive. Cheaper options are Lavender, Neroli and Frankincense. Oils can be used individually or in combination, and only a small quantity of oil is needed. It helps to consult a trained aromatherapist or read some good books on the subject to ensure that you are using the oils safely and in appropriate amounts.

3] Relax and meditate in this area even before you begin your exercises of psychic development. You can do this by sitting comfortably, closing your eyes and breathing deeply. To still your busy mind it may help you to focus upon the movement of your breath, in and out, and to count each exhalation.

4] Surround yourself with a few items that you find beautiful and inspirational: some flowers, perhaps, or a picture of a beautiful landscape. Choose whatever is meaningful for you.

5] When you plan to sit in this place it is ideal to make sure that the lighting is soft. Harsh, glaring lights are not always conducive to relaxation and can distract the mind away from the state of internal contemplation that is helpful for psychic development. This is why some people choose to meditate or do psychic work to the light of a candle, though softer electric light or gentle daylight is also fine.

LEARNING TO RELAX AND MEDITATE

There are many different ways to meditate. Numerous spiritual or religious traditions have their own wonderful meditation practices, but there are many misconceptions about the 'right' way to do it. From my experience of teaching methods of relaxation, meditation and healing, I have discovered that those people who are just willing to play with the techniques and ideas suggested and who do not try too hard to get it right are usually the ones who have the best results. It helps to begin each meditation exercise with a positive intention of what you would like to achieve, and then just trust your mind to travel in whatever direction it needs to go throughout the process. Sometimes our thoughts need to turn to the details and the dramas that surround us so that we can review and release them before settling into a deeper state of relaxation.

At its simplest, meditation can be divided into two categories. The first kind of meditation is concerned with engendering a level of stillness and tranquillity by giving the mind something to concentrate on that distracts it away from the thoughts and illusions of everyday life. A simple example of this is the use of the breathing technique that I have suggested in the Sacred Space Exercise above. The second kind of meditation is more directional, offering particular thoughts, scenarios and visualizations to stimulate specific forms of mental and emotional activity as well as engendering relaxation. Both kinds of meditation are helpful in the development of psychic potential and both are aided by deep breathing and a conscious choice to slow down your rate of inhalation and, more importantly, exhalation.

The meditations that I have created for your psychic development in the following chapters of this book are predominantly directional in nature. They are written for you to guide yourself through a set of ideas, concepts and visualizations that will stimulate your psychic senses. It would be helpful to begin each of these exercises with a couple of minutes' gentle deep breathing and a conscious decision to relax and settle your mind before proceeding. You could imagine that each thought that enters your mind turns into a beautiful bird or butterfly before flying away, leaving you feeling calm, clear and still.

Once you have calmed your thoughts a little, read through the details of the meditation exercise a couple of times to get the general idea of it, then close your eyes and relax back, trusting your mind to take you wherever you need to go. It is not essential to get every detail correct or in the right order for these meditations and exercises to work for you. If you prefer, you could get a trusted friend to guide you through the meditation or you could record your own voice slowly reading it aloud so that you can use the tape to guide you, over and over again. For now, let us begin by preparing the ground for the development of your psychic potential.

A Simple Meditation to Prepare the Ground

- Sit or lie down comfortably in your sacred space. For most people it is best to be upright for this, but if your back will be more comfortable in a horizontal position and you are not the kind of person who is likely to drift off into sleep then you could choose to lie down. Either way, make sure that your back is properly supported and that you keep your body open, with your arms and legs uncrossed. If you are physically open then you are more likely to be mentally and emotionally open for psychic development.

- Once you are comfortable, allow your eyes to close and begin by taking in long, slow, deep breaths; filling your lungs completely but gently, holding for a moment, before slowly releasing the air once again.

- In your mind, hold the thought that you are willing to develop your psychic potential and release any fears, doubts or negative expectations that you may have, imagining all of those misapprehensions harmlessly dissolving into a haze of transformational golden light. Imagine yourself surrounded by protective light energy as you proceed with the exercises within this book, and tell yourself that you are completely safe.

- Next, picture yourself standing in front of a golden doorway that glows with positive energy. There is a smell of fresh flowers; the sound of beautiful, high-pitched chimes gently massages your inner hearing. The feeling of this place is bright and inviting; instinctively you know that you are standing on the threshold of your unique psychic and spiritual potential.

- When you are ready, visualize yourself stepping through this doorway and finding yourself on the other side, bathed in an even brighter golden light and filled with a warm glow of comfort and support. The sounds and smells become sweeter still. Imagine that there is a solid surface beneath your feet and picture yourself relaxing so that your full weight is upon it. Gain a feeling of security and stability from beneath you.

- Stay here for a while, enjoying the feeling of this place and, if you receive any particular ideas, insights, visions or sensations, just notice them and perhaps choose to make a note of them once you have completed the exercise.

- To complete this process, gently stretch your body and open your eyes, sitting quietly for a few moments before proceeding with your activities.

SOME DECLARATIONS FOR SAFE AND EASY PSYCHIC DEVELOPMENT

Within Chapter 2 I discuss the use of affirmational thought to support you in the development of your psychic potential. In the chapters that follow I have included many positive declarations to aid you in developing specific psychic abilities. To begin this process, read this first set of declarations over and over to yourself, repeating them in your mind to guide you forward.

- IT IS SAFE FOR ME TO DEVELOP MY PSYCHIC POTENTIAL.

- MY PROCESS OF PSYCHIC AWAKENING IS EASY, JOYFUL AND PLEASURABLE.

- MY PSYCHIC ABILITIES GROW IN STRENGTH AND STABILITY.

- I TRUST MYSELF AND I TRUST MY INTUITION.

- I LISTEN TO MY INSTINCTS AND ACT UPON THEM WITH LOVE AND COMPASSION.

chapter two

INTUITION AND IMAGINATION

PUSHING OUT THE BOUNDARIES
OF YOUR INTUITION

The abilities commonly described as psychic gifts are simply natural extensions of our intuition. We have all experienced times when our intuition is acute and we are able to listen to it and respond accordingly. Your intuition tells you that it would be a good time to telephone a friend; you have a 'gut feeling' that she is in need of some support and, before you have walked across the room to pick up the telephone, it starts ringing. Your friend has beaten you to it and is telephoning you!

You always park your car in the same spot, under a shady tree just outside your place of work. On one morning, for no explicable reason, you have an instinct to park on the opposite side of the street, still in view from your office window but a little further away than normal. During the day there is a thunderstorm and a heavy branch breaks away from the tree and comes crashing down on the spot where your car would normally have been positioned. At the end of the day you are able to drive home with your windscreen and your paint work still intact!

There are numerous examples of good choices that we make through listening effectively to our intuition. We have so many hunches, coincidences and happy accidents that we do not even notice them half the time, and many such experiences are easily forgotten in our attempts to keep up with the frenetic pace of modern life. When we talk of instinct, hunches and gut feelings we are often referring to one distinct area of psychic awareness: the skills of clairsentience.

Clairsentience is possibly the most commonly developed and, at the same time, the least recognized and acknowledged of all psychic abilities. Even for those of us who are more visually attuned and potentially clairvoyant or who most easily receive information in the form of clairaudient sounds, words and messages, clairsentience is an excellent place to start when we embark upon the adventure of developing our psychic and intuitive gifts. Good clairsentient awareness is also a huge asset for anyone working within the caring professions. It has proved to be essential for many of the healers, counsellors and therapists I have known.

If we push out the boundaries of our gut intuition and learn to sharpen our ability to notice and respond to all of our instincts, then we create a firm foundation for the development of all other psychic skills. Our inner voices, visions and perceptions will be automatically supported and enhanced by our ability to feel, touch and grasp the emotional 'reality' of any given event or situation. For instance, when we walk into an unfamiliar environment for the first time, it is often the feeling of the place that dictates our initial response to it and indicates whether or not we are likely to be comfortable there.

When I work as a healer and counsellor I sometimes utilize my ability to see the auric field around the person with whom I am working. I am often able to see the subtle electro-magnetic field that is emanating from my client, in the form of coloured light. This can give me a range of valuable information which I can use to support the person in the process of self-healing. However, to interpret the information that I am receiving visually it is important for me to listen to my feelings and utilize the physical and emotional response that comes with a developed clairsentient awareness. Indeed, in many cases I receive and act upon the 'gut' information first, before I focus on the visual sense.

During this chapter we will be exploring some ideas, exercises and practical techniques to extend and enhance our clairsentient awareness. As with all of the exercises within this book, when practised they may facilitate the development of all our other senses at the same time, particularly in the areas of intuitive and psychic ability which are already more naturally developed.

IT'S ALL IN THE MIND!

We often dismiss our psychic abilities by telling ourselves that we are imagining things. Many of us regard our imagination as something that is unreal or illusory. We have been taught that the mind plays tricks on us. In numerous cases, highly imaginative children are told not to tell lies by their parents and teachers, leaving them unable to utilize the positive power of the imagination that they were born with. True, we all need to learn to be discerning and rational, but this needs to go hand in hand with the development of intuitive thought, emotional response and imaginative play. A well-developed imagination provides us with an effective bridge to valuable psychic information as well as an abundance of creative energy and ability.

To develop psychically you need to give yourself permission to dream, fantasize and play before allowing your rational mind to do the necessary job of sorting, assessing and figuring out how to act upon the information that you receive. Many of us rationalize or criticize too quickly, without giving our intuition the time and space it deserves. This is just a habit that we have learned and, if we choose, we can easily replace it with a different habit that is healthier, more creative and much more effective for developing accurate intuition.

DAILY DECLARATIONS

To give yourself permission to use your imagination constructively and to open your mind, body and emotions to greater clairsentient ability, I have created some daily declarations for you to use. These daily declarations are similar to those at the end of Chapter 1. They are simple but powerful positive affirmations that gently help to alter your beliefs, habits and expectations from those which may be less conducive to the development of your intuitive awareness to those which are much more so.

Within the following chapters there are some more daily declarations which have been tailored to help you develop specific sensory skills, but the collection I have included below will always be valuable to you regardless of your unique psychic and intuitive abilities. The development of your 'gut' awareness will always support your clairvoyant, clairaudient and healing abilities.

The additional benefit of these daily declarations when used on a regular basis is that, like all positive affirmations, they will help to make you more available for some experiences and less available for others. For example, if you regularly affirm that it is safe for you to develop your psychic abilities, then the experience of life you are most likely to have is one where you always feel safe and stable as you grow into your psychic awareness. The power of declaration is strong: what we ask for, we often receive.

HOW TO USE YOUR DAILY DECLARATIONS

As a general guideline, the more you use these declarations the more effective they will be in supporting your process of development. However, even if you use them a little they will still benefit you in subtle ways by clarifying your intention and making you more available for the support of positive psychic guides and energies. Just holding on to the idea that there are supportive influences available to you, asking for help when you need it and utilizing positive declarations of your intent will greatly ease your progress.

MORNING AND EVENING DECLARATIONS

Develop a habit of using your daily declarations first thing when you wake up and last thing before you go to sleep. Keep a list of them beside your bed and do your best to memorize them for use at other times throughout the day.

You can say them to yourself out loud, hearing the sound and feeling the vibration of your voice, or repeat them silently in your head, listening to the inner sound of your thoughts and feelings as you do so. Alternatively, you could write them down, type them out, sing them, chant them or record yourself saying them and play yourself a tape of the declarations at regular intervals. If you are a particularly visual person, write or paint them in bright colours and paste them on to doors, mirrors, the refrigerator and other places where they will be constantly visible to you.

DECLARATION IN COMBINATION

Throughout the day you can repeat your declarations to yourself in combination with other activities such as exercising, walking to your place of work, doing the washing up or practising relaxation techniques and meditation. Whatever you do as part of your daily routine, there are bound to be activities which do not fully engage your mind and which can be combined in some way with the use of declarations.

It is perhaps particularly valuable to combine the use of your daily declarations with many of the other exercises, techniques and meditations I have created for you in this book. You could choose four or five appropriate declarations to repeat a couple of times over as you settle down to meditate, then repeat them once again as you complete the process.

The whole concept of positive thought and declaration is an interesting area to explore. Indeed, the use of positive thought techniques to heal and enhance other areas of our lives, such as our relationships and our physical well-being, appears to have a positive, knock-on effect on psychic development. For more detailed information about the construction and use of positive affirmations for health, well-being and success, you may wish to refer to my book *Principles of Self-healing*. For now, here are some appropriate declarations, read them through slowly to yourself once or twice and begin to use them straight away.

DAILY DECLARATIONS FOR INTUITIVE AWARENESS

- IT IS SAFE FOR ME TO DEVELOP MY INTUITION.

- MY INTUITIVE AWARENESS GROWS IN STRENGTH AND SENSITIVITY.

- I TRUST THE POWER OF MY IMAGINATION.

- I EASILY HARNESS AND UTILIZE MY PSYCHIC GIFTS.

- I AM A CREATIVE, IMAGINATIVE AND INTUITIVE PERSON.

DAILY DECLARATIONS FOR CLAIRSENTIENCE

- IT IS SAFE FOR ME TO DEVELOP MY CLAIRSENTIENCE.

- I TRUST MY 'GUT' FEELINGS AND REACTIONS.

- IT IS EASY FOR ME TO ACT UPON MY CLAIRSENTIENT ABILITIES.

- MY INSTINCTS ARE VALUABLE, EFFECTIVE AND HIGHLY DEVELOPED.

- I AM A POWERFULLY CLAIRSENTIENT PERSON.

THE MIND WITHIN THE BODY

The terms 'gut' feeling or 'gut' intuition are not accidental ones. The area of the body between the heart and the groin which encompasses the stomach and solar plexus is particularly sensitive and could be said to have its own intelligence. Indeed, the stomach and solar plexus contain two of the seven main energy centres or chakras that are integral to the teachings of the Indian Yogic system as discussed in Chapter 3 (*see diagram page 55*). What is more, on a physiological level this region of the body contains a mass of nerve-endings and, while it is quite different, it could be said that it rivals the area of the brain in its complexity. Is it possible that each of us has a brain in our body as well as in our head, and that we have a body-mind or body-intelligence to match?

Certainly as a hands-on healer and a counsellor who teaches self-healing techniques I would have no hesitation in asserting that the body has its own intelligence which can be employed and stimulated for healing to occur. It would make sense for each of us to develop that body-intelligence at an extra-sensory level to bring us guidance, inspiration and clear information about our own state of health and the well-being of others.

When I give hands-on healing I often help my clients to develop a special dialogue between themselves and their own unique physical intelligence. I guide them into a state of relaxation, and channel healing energy through my hands, my voice, my heart and my mind. Within my own body I frequently receive an impression of my clients' physical state. I register the location of blocked, overactive or depleted energy in my clients' body and I encourage them to explore that part of their anatomy. Often they will develop a clear impression of what their body needs to help restore itself, and together we can work with that information to stimulate positive change. Sometimes the solution is purely physical but often it is a combination of physical, emotional, mental and spiritual approaches that produces the best results. Information about the best path to healing is usually forthcoming when both the healer and the person seeking help can consult their individual body-intelligence and 'gut' awareness.

It is in the gut that we tend to experience pleasure and pain; the pleasure of being loved and accepted, perhaps, or the pain of loss or rejection. It is also in the gut that we often experience a feeling for the environment we are in or the people we meet. Walking into a house with an unsettled atmosphere may leave us with an unsettled feeling in the pit of our stomach, while meeting a person who is genuinely kind, honest, friendly and pleased to see us will invariably leave us with a warm glow that is quite tangible.

Meditation: Stimulating 'Gut' Awareness

- Find somewhere quiet and comfortable to sit, unplug the telephone and make sure that you are not going to be disturbed. Sit with your back supported and your body open and relaxed, your arms and legs uncrossed. If you prefer you can lie down for this, but again make sure that you keep your body open rather than curled up.

- I am going to invite you to use some positive mental images. Some people have strong images when they do this, some haven't. For this exercise to work for you, it is enough just to hold the idea, feeling or concept in your mind.

- So to begin, breathe deeply, allowing every breath to fill your lungs completely without straining, and then slowly exhaling. Take a couple of minutes to notice the feeling of your breath as it moves in and out of your body and then gently allow it to assume its own deep rhythm for a while.

- Imagine that the area of your solar plexus (just below the centre of your rib cage) and stomach contains a powerful mind that steadily vibrates with the impulses from its own intelligence, awareness and sensitivity. Every physical sensation, feeling and emotion exists as a ripple of awareness from this extraordinary body-mind.

- Imagine yourself breathing directly into your body-mind, the breath from your lungs easily connecting you to your physical and emotional intelligence. As you do this, be aware of stimulating a stronger relationship between this part of yourself and your conscious awareness so that you are always attuned to the power of your gut instinct. What are the feelings that you sense within your body at this time? What are your emotions telling you? Are you feeling calm, excited, sad, joyful, turbulent, peaceful, passionate, angry or loving? Do your best to notice all of your physical and emotional sensations and accept them, allowing them to ebb and flow in their own way and at their own pace.

- Next, imagine your solar plexus and stomach filling with coloured light that is reminiscent of bright sunshine. Ripples of clear yellow, vibrant orange, shimmering red and fresh, light gold gently penetrate this area, bringing softness, warmth and illumination. The coloured lights are accompanied by rippling sounds of beautiful chimes and a soft, pulsing heartbeat percussion that creates a greater sense of ease within your body. Breathe deeply and allow yourself to experience a feeling of expansion as your stomach muscles relax and waves of energy spread from there to stimulate and calm every area of your body.

- Sense the energy of this light, sound and feeling touching you deeply to awaken the extrasensory power that is available to you through this area of your body. Your 'gut' awareness is healed and stimulated to receive positive sensual information. Your innate clairsentience is strengthened and enhanced. Again, notice any particular feelings or sensations that you receive at this time. Does your body have a message for you? Are there any insights contained within your emotions? Just notice without expectation or judgement and accept what you feel.

- When you are ready to complete this exercise, visualize a shield of copper and gold that runs, three hundred and sixty degrees, around your body from just below your heart to just above your groin. Know that you can dissolve this shield whenever you choose to, but that in the meantime it provides you with solidity, stability, protection and a feeling of security as you continue to expand into greater intuitive awareness.

Meditation: The High Priest or Priestess

Our normal perception of ourselves, although often comforting and secure, can sometimes restrict our potential for development. We get used to seeing ourselves as a particular kind of person, fulfilling certain roles and allowing ourselves to be defined by the jobs that we do or by the needs and opinions of other people. Utilizing the powers of the imagination we can see ourselves in different guises and role-play exciting new possibilities that we may have previously discounted. Perceiving ourselves in new ways can help to stimulate new abilities, allowing us to model our development upon our dreams and desires.

This 'fantasy' meditation will allow you to explore your clairsentient potential and help you to develop beyond previous boundaries and limitations. As this is quite a long meditation, you may wish to record it so that you can be guided slowly through it by your own voice without having to memorize it all or read it as you go.

- Once again, find somewhere quiet and comfortable to sit, unplug the telephone and make sure that you are not going to be disturbed. Sit or lie down with your back supported and your body open and relaxed, your arms and legs uncrossed.

- Breathe deeply and imagine that you are living on a paradise island, far distant from your current environment. The weather, although varied, is generally warm and clement and the air is filled with fragrant breezes perfumed with the essences of honey, flowers and spice. Picture yourself living in a cave that is filled with rich fabrics, beautiful shells, shimmering crystals and soft, cushioned furniture made from exotic wood.

- During the day you are free to roam the beaches and forests of this island, tuning in to the sounds and senses of nature. You hear the calls of numerous exquisite birds as they fly, perch and stretch their iridescent feathers in the sunlight. In your heart and solar plexus you can feel the impulses of their joy, freedom and quest for survival as they forage for food, court their mates and nest in the boughs of magnificent trees.

- Through your feet you can feel the subtle vibrations of the earth, echoes of the heartbeat at the core of the planet. Every grain of sand, every stone and every patch of rich, dark loam sends its messages of peace, stability and power to touch you in the depths of your stomach. Your hands and arms brush past the leaves of lush plants that send welcoming ripples of intelligent curiosity and soothing contact into the cells of your body.

- In the evenings you return to your cave to eat, wash in a nearby spring and adorn yourself in rich fabrics festooned with the colours of the birds and trees. You become the high priest or priestess of this island paradise, making yourself available to all who respectfully seek your powerful clairsentient wisdom.

- You are visited by friendly people who arrive individually or in small groups to receive your blessing and to benefit from your advice. Your instinctive awareness reaches like a loving hand to touch gently the feelings of those who consult you. You sense their hopes and fears, their dreams, desires, passions, concerns and confusions. Your presence calms them and you answer all questions with confidence and compassion, secure in the knowledge that your words of wisdom are aligned to their true nature and greatest spiritual potential. In return they bring you gifts of food, spices and precious minerals.

- Gradually your visitors depart, feeling comforted and healed by your insights and intuition. You are left in the company of one or two good friends who nurture you and laugh with you as you share delicious secrets; telling each other stories about the mysteries and brilliance of the universe. You complete your day gazing at the stars, tuning in to the twinkling vibration of each nocturnal light to coax you into dreams of higher consciousness.

- Knowing that you can repeat this meditation and tune in to this facet of yourself whenever you choose, imagine the sensuality, wisdom, compassion and developed clairsentient ability of this persona returning with you to your normal waking consciousness.

- You are the high priest or priestess of your own destiny; your instincts and intuition guide and protect you always.

SENSING ENVIRONMENTS AND ATMOSPHERES

We all pick up information about any environment we find ourselves in, from the moment we arrive. On a visual level we are influenced by the colours, shapes and styles around us even before we consciously begin to decide whether or not we like the look of a place. The sounds and smells influence us too and, on a more subtle level, every environment may leave us with a particular taste in our mouth, which in some cases can be quite distinctive. Operating alongside our other senses is our kinaesthetic awareness, which responds to the feeling of a door handle and registers an emotional reaction to the atmosphere that exists in the room on the other side of the door. For many of us, this kinaesthetic sense is highly attuned and can give us detailed information about the physical, emotional and energetic nature of any given place.

A room that is loved and cared for will feel quite different to one that is somewhat neglected. There is also a discernible difference between the feeling of a room that is used by people who relate to each other in a harmonious, loving way and that of an environment which has been the focus for resentful, competitive and bitter relationships. Everything that happens within an environment affects the way that it feels to the casual observer and can be effectively registered by an experienced clairsentient who chooses to work with environmental energy.

Practitioners of the art of Feng Shui know a great deal about the need to balance and work constructively with the life-force energy that circulates through and around an environment. Just as a human being can benefit from energetic healing, so can a house, a garden, an office or a public building. With Feng Shui, the placing of certain objects such as mirrors, light fittings, pictures, furniture, ornaments, hanging crystals, plants and screens can help to regulate energy that is out of balance. A balanced environment becomes a healthier, more harmonious and potentially more prosperous place for people to live and work in.

Some clairsentients who develop their ability to work with environments may function in a similar way to Feng Shui practitioners, but rather than follow a particular system they may operate by instinctively knowing how to bring harmony to their surroundings. They may be able to channel a form of healing energy which can raise the vibrational tone of a room, or they may suggest colours, shapes, objects or spiritual practices that can help to transform the feeling of an environment. This is an excellent psychic ability for an architect, decorator, interior designer, housekeeper, cleaner or conference organizer to develop. Indeed, it is beneficial to anyone who regularly creates or provides environments for other people to live, work, study or socialize within.

Good clairsentient awareness of environments can also help to keep us safe. If we walk into a building and receive a gut feeling that there is some kind of disturbance present we can make appropriate choices about our own well-being and about the well-being of anyone within our care. Using clairsentience we may make informed choices about where we live, where we work, where we socialize and how we can best manage or make the most of an environment that is not ideal for us. A combination of good gut instincts, positive thoughts and a confident posture is also the best formula for keeping us safe as we walk down the street, ensuring that we both give and receive the right signals.

This next meditation is a fantasy that is designed to stimulate your environmental awareness.

Meditation: A Drop in the Ocean

- Sit or lie down comfortably with your back supported and your body open and relaxed.

- Breathe deeply and imagine yourself to be a beautiful fish in a tropical ocean. You are brightly coloured and elegantly formed; you glide sensuously through the translucent waters. Enjoy the feelings of freedom and movement as you swim and play. Your body is cradled by the watery substance of this oceanic world.

- Now imagine yourself to be one fish amid a school of many brightly coloured individuals. Picture yourself swimming in synchronous rhythm with your group. You easily feel and sense the mood of the group, experiencing what the group experiences, shifting direction in perfect time and rhythm with all of the others. There is no conscious effort involved in this; you automatically anticipate each subtle fluctuation of feeling and adapt your movements accordingly, negotiating the space around you perfectly.

- Next, imagine yourself to be able to feel and respond to the mood of this entire oceanic world, responding to the changes of tide and rhythm over a wide area. You automatically sense and locate the best areas of the ocean in which to feed, play and swim. Your gut instincts keep you safe by helping you to steer clear of any dangers such as underwater predators or depths wherein the water pressure would be too great for you. Instead, you find the most peaceful places to swim, jewelled with the most beautiful corals and strands of rich seaweed which undulate with the currents. You are in total harmony and fully attuned with your environment.

What would it be like to sense, read and respond to environments this effectively, adapting yourself perfectly to each physical and emotional fluctuation around you? As a human being, sense yourself awakening these intuitive abilities to help you in your life. Your powerful clairsentience supports you in health, happiness and success and guides you to the places that are most suitable for your well-being. Think about the difference this environmental ability is going to make to you and imagine yourself to have already developed a high degree of skill and competence. Learning to use your clairsentience is a natural part of being alive.

Exercise: Exploring a Room

In the main, it will be easier for you to detect feelings and atmospheres in an environment that is unfamiliar to you, as you will necessarily both strongly influence and identify with familiar places, particularly your own home. However, it may be valuable to begin this exercise by practising at home. Then, when you are comfortable with the concept you can practise it anywhere you choose.

- Walk around your chosen room, beginning by noticing what is obvious about it. How light or dark is the room? Where are the light sources? What colours are in the room? What shapes can you see around you? How warm is the room? What sounds can you hear around you? Does the room have a smell? Does this place leave a particular taste in your mouth?

- Next, place one hand on your stomach or solar plexus and notice what you feel in this part of your body as you walk around. Is this area relaxed or tense? Do you have a sensation of comfort within your body or is there a sense of unease? How do you feel emotionally? Does this room engender any particular feeling at this time? Is your physical and emotional state different from how it was before you entered this room? Give yourself plenty of time to do this: feelings are at their most revealing when they are given a reasonable amount of space and when they are listened to intently.

- Ask yourself about the personality of the room and notice your gut responses. What is the function of this room? What kinds of things occur here? Are the people who use this room generally happy with life or is there any discord? Does this room help people to be comfortable and function well within it or not? What has happened here in the past that is still having an influence on the feeling of this room in the present? Trust your gut instincts to give you answers to these questions.

- If this room does not feel completely balanced and harmonious, ask yourself the following questions and just notice the thoughts and feelings that you have: What needs to change to improve the feeling of this environment? Would it benefit from a physical change such as rearranging the furniture, altering the colour scheme or bringing in more light? Does this room need to be used in a more loving and positive manner? Once more, remember to trust your instincts. If you are in an environment that feels particularly disturbed, it may be better not to linger unless you are feeling particularly resilient.

- You may wish to make notes of what you sense in this room and compare your impressions with those you may have in the same location at another time. As with any other ability, the best results come with regular practice.

CLEANSING AND HEALING
YOUR ENVIRONMENT

There are many ways in which you can lighten, brighten, balance and bring healing to an environment. Some time ago I rented out my house for a year so that I could travel to Spain, Ireland, California and the east coast of the US. For part of that time I was teaching, but my main purpose for taking a year away from home was to write my book *Star Healing* without the everyday distractions of living and working in London. On my return I discovered that the tenants who had been living in my house had not taken very good care of it and the building had lost its normal feeling of warmth, peace and clarity.

During the first few weeks after I moved back into my house I did many things to remedy the feelings of imbalance that were present. On a physical level I did plenty of cleaning and tidying. I had the carpets cleaned, I washed down walls and I reorganized my possessions. This process allowed me to cleanse the house of psychic debris as well as the physical dirt, and it helped me to 'claim' the space as mine again. On an intuitive level, I took time to explore my house psychically in the manner described above, feeling out those areas that needed extra care and bringing them to a new state of harmony by using many of the ideas detailed in Chapter 1. The exercise for creating your sacred space (*page 19*) is an effective way of achieving this.

When cleansing and healing an environment it is most important to use the techniques and rituals that hold the most meaning for you. If, for example, lighting candles is more meaningful for you than burning essential oils, then trust yourself and choose to do what is most appropriate for your needs and belief system.

The essential ingredient for all psychic cleansing is to have a positive underlying intention of what you wish to achieve and the techniques you need to support you in this. For myself, I like to use a combination of visual, auditory and kinaesthetic rituals, engaging more than one of my physical and psychic senses in the process of healing environmental energy. I also love to visualize bright, coloured light filling and transforming an area by dissolving or dispersing any disturbance that may be present.

Exercise: Defining the Boundaries

One important consideration when working with environmental energy is to clarify and reaffirm the boundaries of the space in question. If a room, house, garden or office has clearly defined psychic boundaries then it is less likely to be invaded by people whose influence is disrespectful or abusive of the space.

1] Slowly walk around the perimeters of your environment sensing with your body and emotions as before. Imagine these perimeters to be fully protected. Picture them strengthened by a force-field of bright light which repels anything unwanted and attracts everything that is both desired and spiritually appropriate for those who live or work within this space. If you prefer, you could imagine a force-field of sound, fragrance or sensation as well as the field of light. You could have an energy field of clear, light chimes, the fragrance of honeysuckle or the feeling of velvet or wood bark. Be inventive and use sensual images that feel appropriate to you or to the people who use this space.

Many people like to walk the perimeters of an environment holding a lighted candle, singing, chanting, banging a drum or burning fragrant incense or a smudge stick of sage and cedar. Once again, use whatever feels appropriate to you.

2] Notice where the physical boundaries of your environment need repair or renovation and pay particular attention to these areas. If it is possible for you to undertake physical repairs or instruct the owner of the environment to do so, then that would be ideal, but in the meantime it would be helpful to start by mentally rebuilding and renovating. This 'mental maintenance' creates a specific psychic field which will help to keep these areas protected and may also speed up the physical maintenance that is to follow. Its purpose is similar to boarding up a broken window while you wait for a new pane of glass to be cut. While it is not ideal long term, it will temporarily help to create greater comfort and security. Mentally imagine walls being rebuilt, fences constructed, gates hung and well oiled, flooring resealed, roof tiles replaced and bolts fitted.

3] Place 'psychic markers' at key points around the perimeters of the environment. Many animals do this with scent, methodically staking out the perimeters of their territory on a regular basis. You could do this by imagining lights or flares at each corner of a building or a garden and at each door, gate and window. Alternatively, picture yourself painting and putting up signs at significant points. Choose to imagine the signs with positive and appropriate wording. It is better to place more focus upon what you wish to attract to the environment rather than what you wish to repel. For example, 'This environment welcomes only positive, loving people, positive, rewarding experiences, good health, happiness and prosperity.' Visualize the signs written in bright colours or even fluorescent lighting; as always, be creative.

GUT INSTINCTS ABOUT OTHER PEOPLE

We often know a lot about other people from our first meeting and a considerable amount of what we first discern turns out to be incredibly accurate. However, at the beginning of a relationship we also tend to pre-judge people based upon our past relationships and experiences, so there can be a blurred line between fearful misconceptions and good clairsentient information. There is no absolute formula for discerning the difference between prejudice and sound intuition, but with regular practice and a willingness to let go of judgemental thinking we can all learn to clarify our first impressions of others.

It is generally healthier to be willing to take a positive view of other people in the first instance and only alter that view if we receive strong indications to the contrary. We are more likely to find positive qualities in other people if we look for them rather than fearfully looking only for the worst. However, always listen to your gut feelings and the impulses of your heart. Sometimes you will receive an immediate sense that it is safe to get close to another person or at least, to work with them. If, on the contrary, you receive warning signals then you do need to respect your instincts.

It is important that psychics and healers do not work closely with people they have a strong adverse reaction to. Just because someone asks for help or advice does not mean that we always have to oblige. This does not necessarily mean that these individuals are bad people. Sometimes we receive adverse feelings when our gut instincts are telling us that we do not have the energy or the experience to work with certain people and that they would be better served by working with somebody else. On other occasions our instincts may tell us that the person in question is not in a position to make constructive use of what we have to offer and that we would be wasting time and resources that would be better channelled elsewhere.

Receiving clairsentient information about another person is more than just a positive or negative reaction, however; rather than flat shapes of black or white, this information takes the form of a whole landscape of colours, textures, feelings and sensations. Once you have chosen to get close to someone and develop a personal relationship with him or her, or once you have established an ongoing working relationship, you will sense different kinds of information as that person, and you, move through a variety of moods, feelings and experiences.

When I have lived with other people I have often picked up accurate information about their moods and experiences from a distance. Often when I have been at home I have felt the mood of the person I have been living with enter the house before she or he has even walked through the front door. When one friend had been involved in a minor road accident I felt his distress like a punch in the stomach a few minutes before he arrived back home. Similarly, I have perceived feelings of joy, sadness, excitement, loss, love and warmth before the person who is experiencing them has physically walked into the room. We all radiate a vast amount of information about ourselves and the experiences that have left an impression on us.

When I work with people one-to-one or in groups I can often sense their moving landscape of feelings. Also, I frequently sense their special qualities, gifts and hidden potential. I am not unique in this, we all operate with a level of clairsentient ability that helps to keep us safe and to relate appropriately to the people around us. Healers, counsellors and good psychics utilize this clairsentient information to help them give relevant emotional guidance to their clients and support others to make the most of their talents and abilities.

Exercise: Exploring a Person

This exercise is the basis of all psychic work involving other people. Here the emphasis is on clairsentient information, but the same principles can be applied to working clairvoyantly, clairaudiently or in many other ways.

It would be best to do this exercise with a friend who is also wishing to develop her or his intuition, but once you are comfortable with the concept you can subtly practise noticing the feelings and sensations you perceive as you meet people socially or through work.

- To begin, sit opposite your partner. You need to make sure that you are sitting quite close to each other while assuming a comfortable position that is easy to maintain. Hold hands with your partner and close your eyes. Remain silent and focus on your feelings rather than the impressions that you receive visually or through your hearing. This does not mean that you ignore clairvoyant or clairaudient information. Rather, it is important for you consciously to bring your attention to the feelings of your heart, solar plexus and stomach, and to notice the sensations that you experience in other parts of your body too.

- With your partner, breathe deeply. It often helps to synchronize your breathing for a few repetitions so that you breathe in rhythm and harmony with each other as you relax. Then, allowing your breath to assume its normal depth and pace, begin to sense information about the other person. As this is a two-way exercise, your partner will also be doing the same with you. Where in your own body are you feeling relaxed? Is there any tension anywhere? What feelings move through you as you reach out your clairsentient awareness towards your partner? What qualities does this person possess? What is she or he feeling? What does this person need at this time?

- If your partner is a good friend you will probably know a great deal about him or her and the impressions that you receive may confirm what you are already aware of, but take the opportunity to explore any other feelings that are there. Take plenty of time for this: some feelings move more slowly than others and it is good to go beyond the more superficial impressions that you receive and give yourself the space to sense deeper information. I would suggest a minimum of 15 minutes and a maximum of an hour when you first begin to do this. Later, you may receive so much information that you may choose to take longer over this exercise.

- After a while, open your eyes and share the information that you and your partner have received. If you have any particular insights for each other, share those too and make a note of anything valuable. Deliver all information as positively as you can and be sensitive to each other's privacy and space. If you have tapped into an area that your partner is unable or unwilling to discuss, for whatever reason, move on to some of the other impressions that you had. However, if you or your partner have been correct in an impression about something that you have not previously discussed, it would be good if you could give each other some confirmation of success even if you choose not to go into details.

- I have known some people feel aware of very little when they first do this, but then once they open their mouth to speak they discover that they have received more information about their partner than they initially realized. Like any other ability it may take practice to notice the full range of information available to you, so take heart if the process seems slow in the beginning. Remember that it is all right to make mistakes and that it is usually worth the risk of sharing information which you would normally put down to an 'over-active imagination'. Your imagination is the bridge to your higher senses.

- To complete the exercise, consciously separate from your partner by moving away from each other and imagining a safety curtain of white light, bright sounds and warm feelings between you, providing you with a natural boundary. Imagine yourself harmlessly breathing out all the feelings that are not yours and that do not belong to you, releasing them safely into the atmosphere to be dissolved with healing light.

THE EXPANSION OF SENSORY AWARENESS

The time that you spend on your psychic development will undoubtedly have an impact upon your physical senses as well as your psychic ones. You may suddenly become aware of a whole range of feelings, sensations, tastes, smells, sounds, visions and experiences that you had not previously been available for. To complete this chapter I would like to offer you some daily declarations to aid your sensory awareness and help to direct it positively and constructively.

DAILY DECLARATIONS FOR SENSORY EXPANSION

- MY AWARENESS DEVELOPS IN NEW AND EXCITING WAYS EVERY DAY.

- MY IMAGINATION IS THE BRIDGE TO NEW AWARENESS.

- ALL OF MY SENSES ARE GROWING AND EXPANDING.

- I ALWAYS GROW INTO JOY, ECSTASY AND FREEDOM.

- I OPEN THE DOORS TO MANY WONDERFUL NEW EXPERIENCES AND PERCEPTIONS.

chapter three

YOUR HIGHER VISION

YOUR MIND'S EYE

We often hear people describe psychic ability as clairvoyance. The word 'clairvoyant' is perhaps the term most commonly used to describe anyone with a pronounced psychic ability, and particularly to describe someone who gives psychic readings or 'sittings' on a professional basis. To be more accurate, clairvoyance describes a range of psychic abilities based upon a developed visual sense. The literal meaning of clairvoyance is 'clear sight' or 'clear vision'. A true clairvoyant will receive psychic messages or information through a heightened visual awareness.

Similar to people with a profound psychic ability in other areas, many clairvoyants will also have a range of other psychic skills (such as clairaudience, clairsentience) but their predominant source of information will tend to be visual. The tendency for all of us, whatever our special skills, is to use our most developed sense first and foremost, while our other senses back up our first impressions and help us to interpret what we perceive.

Throughout this chapter we will explore some different kinds of clairvoyant ability and some other aspects of visual awareness; I will be offering you some exercises to awaken and strengthen your innate clairvoyance. These would be useful to practise even if your innate psychic abilities are not predominantly visual. If we exercise a set of muscles, then they can support our overall strength and fitness even if they are not the muscles that we use the most. Similarly, with psychic awareness developing one sense will support our overall ability to receive and act upon useful information.

SUBJECTIVE CLAIRVOYANCE

By far the most commonly experienced form of clairvoyance is the ability to receive visual information internally. Most of us have had the experience of conjuring up an image in our mind's eye when we are remembering a past event or when we are asked to imagine what something we have not seen first-hand looks like. Those of us who are particularly visual will regularly recall, perceive and imagine things in this way. Many clairvoyants receive psychic information in a similar fashion, perceiving visual images, symbols and impressions within their mind's eye which they then interpret accordingly. This ability is sometimes described as 'subjective' clairvoyance.

This subjective clairvoyant ability is particularly common among people who can easily visualize and who are blessed with an imagination that favours visual signals. Some subjective clairvoyants may even develop as psychic artists because they have such a strong, natural ability to copy or translate their inner pictures into tangible form onto canvas or paper. Some can even translate them into three-dimensional images or sculptures. This area will be explored further in Chapter 6.

Most subjective clairvoyants receive visual information through what is often described as *the third eye*. The third eye is one of the seven main chakras or energy centres detailed in the teachings of the Indian Yogic tradition. These chakras are bridges between the physical body and the subtle 'electricity' of the non-physical, esoteric and auric bodies that make up the human energetic system. The third eye or 'brow' chakra is located at the centre of the forehead and is given its name because it is able to receive subtle visual information in an apparently similar manner to the way that the physical eyes receive tangible information from the surrounding environment. The other six main chakras follow the line of the spinal column and are located at the base of the spine, the abdomen, the solar plexus, the heart, the throat, and the crown (a few inches above the head).

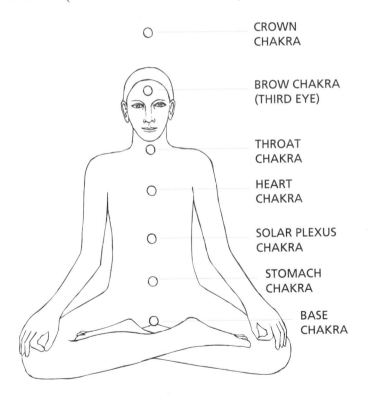

CROWN
CHAKRA

BROW CHAKRA
(THIRD EYE)

THROAT
CHAKRA

HEART
CHAKRA

SOLAR PLEXUS
CHAKRA

STOMACH
CHAKRA

BASE
CHAKRA

Subjective clairvoyant messages can come in the form of lights, colours, cinematic images or abstract symbols, seen or perceived in the area of the forehead. However, some clairvoyants describe the images that they see as being projected forward from their third eye, as if there were a television or cinema screen a few inches in front of their forehead. In the case of someone who is highly visual, the images may even appear to be quite three-dimensional and have a quality similar to a sophisticated holographic picture which can be viewed from more than one angle.

Like all psychics, subjective clairvoyants may receive information from their own higher mind or higher awareness, spirit guides, other people (in the form of telepathic communications), environmental influences and numerous other sources which we can only theorize about. We all have the potential to develop subjective clairvoyance, although, as previously discussed, many of us will have greater natural abilities that relate to our other psychic senses. However, we can all benefit from exercising our 'inner eye' and awakening our higher vision. Here are some daily declarations and meditations to help you.

DAILY DECLARATIONS FOR CLAIRVOYANT VISION

- IT IS EASY FOR ME TO VISUALIZE.

- I AM WILLING TO RECEIVE VISUAL INFORMATION.

- IT IS SAFE AND EASY FOR ME TO OPEN AND CLOSE MY INNER EYE.

- I EASILY DEVELOP A POWERFUL AND EFFECTIVE CLAIRVOYANT ABILITY.

- I AM WILLING TO RECEIVE CLAIRVOYANT SYMBOLS AND MESSAGES.

Meditation: Opening Your Inner Eye

- Find somewhere quiet and comfortable to sit, unplug the telephone and make sure that you are not going to be disturbed. Sit with your back supported and your body open and relaxed, your arms and legs uncrossed. If you prefer you can lie down for this, but again make sure that you keep your body open rather than curled up.

- As before, I am going to invite you to use some positive mental images. Some people have strong images when they do this and some haven't. For this exercise to work for you, it is enough just to hold the idea or concept in your mind.

- So to begin, breathe deeply and focus on the area of your third eye in the centre of your forehead. Imagine it as a physical eye, similar to your other eyes below it; visualize it with its eyelid softly closed for peaceful rest and protection. When you are ready, picture your whole forehead area bathed with the gentle golden light of psychic awareness, and then imagine your third eye beginning to open in a way that is similar to a flower opening its petals to the soft morning sunshine.

- Notice how clear and beautiful your third eye is. What colour does the pupil of your eye appear to be? If you do not immediately see a colour then make a guess and use your imagination to paint it with your preferred hue. Continue to visualize your eye bathed with a soft golden light and feel it growing stronger, your vision becoming clearer and more perceptive. Hold the idea that your inner eye is completely healthy and is constantly expanding its ability to receive clairvoyant information.

- Be aware of any thoughts, feelings and sensations that you have as you do this. If you have already begun to receive some mental pictures, symbols or impressions of light, then your clairvoyant sense may already be operating. Equally, the opening of your third eye may have stimulated one or more of your other psychic senses, so it is valuable that you observe what is happening to you. Make a mental note of what you see, hear, feel and experience, perhaps writing down any ideas or inspirations once the meditation is complete.

- To complete this meditation, bathe your third eye with a light of deep indigo blue to protect it, heal it and keep it safe, then imagine the eyelid softly closing again, cushioning the eye from external influences.

Repeat this exercise on a regular basis, spending some time in a relaxed, receptive, contemplative state to allow for any visual information to be transmitted to you from your higher mind or from some external source. It would be particularly useful to practise this last thing at night, before you go to sleep. Always complete this process in the same way, by bathing the eye with indigo light and closing the eyelid as above.

PROTECTING YOUR INNER VISION

It is as important to remember to close down your clairvoyant vision as it is to open it. Good, sustainable and healthy clairvoyant perception comes from an ability to be able to open and shut our inner eye at will. To some extent, this comes naturally to us all: we automatically switch off our psychic vision when we do not need it or when we need to protect ourselves from receiving too much information. However, some people, when they develop their psychic abilities, tend to concentrate too much on opening and expanding their awareness and forget to put an equal amount of energy into strengthening their capability to direct the flow of psychic information. This is a bit like having the front door of your house propped open 24 hours a day. It is fine if we live somewhere where the weather is always warm and dry or where we have no need to secure our home, but most people would have a good reason to shut their front door for at least part of the day.

In some cases, a door or gate that is constantly open can lose its ability to shut easily when required: the hinges rust or seize up from lack of use. Something similar happens in the case of psychic awareness: leaving our inner doors and windows open may affect their flexibility and ease of movement. Consciously shutting down your clairvoyant abilities after you have consciously opened them keeps your hinges oiled and allows you to discriminate between appropriate and inappropriate use of your clairvoyance.

Once you have practised opening and closing your inner eye a few times in the manner described above, you may wish to move on to the following meditation.

Meditation: Opening the Inner Membranes
• Once again, find a quiet, comfortable place to meditate; sit or lie down with your back supported and your body open and relaxed.

- Focus on the area of your third eye at the centre of your forehead. Picture your whole forehead area bathed with the gentle golden light of psychic awareness, then imagine your third eye beginning to open as before.

- Once it is open, imagine that your third eye has a series of inner lids or subtle membranes. These delicate membranes are virtually invisible but they are also strong and robust, allowing them to protect your inner vision effectively, whenever required. Picture the first membrane opening to allow in more light and vision. Notice any images, feelings, thoughts and impressions, then proceed to open the second membrane and beyond.

- Continue to open up one membrane or lid after another in an infinite cycle, pausing every few seconds to notice anything new. You could visualize this process as opening up more and more petals on a lotus flower or a chrysanthemum. Make a mental note of anything that occurs no matter how minor and subtle it may appear to be. As you progress, imagine that your eye is able to perceive more light, greater beauty, more wisdom and more peace as each lid opens. To complete, bathe the eye with a light of deep indigo blue to protect it, heal it and keep it safe and then imagine the membranes and eyelids (or petals) easily closing as before.

- Alternatively, imagine yourself gently removing veils, curtains or clouds of soft mist from around your physical eyes and your inner one. Imagine light, inspiration and information shining into your mind before placing a protective veil of indigo blue around your head to complete the process.

REGULAR SITTINGS

As with clairsentient ability, the best way to develop your clairvoyance is to sit in meditation or quiet contemplation on a regular basis and practise being available for clairvoyant information. You could do this on your own, with a support partner who is also wishing to develop her or his clairvoyant ability, or with a small support group of like-minded people.

Many people find that regularity is a key element to the success of their sittings. Taking 10 to 20 minutes at roughly the same time every day or every couple of days to be alone, sit and relax can set up a rhythm that may support your psychic development. Similarly, meeting with your support partner or support group for a couple of hours on the same evening every week and at a similar time can be a helpful way of supporting the combined intention of the individuals involved to develop sound clairvoyant vision. However, there are no hard-and-fast rules about this; each of us needs to develop in ways that are comfortable for us and that are congruent with all of the other commitments and interests that we have. Sitting on any given day and at any time of the day, once or twice every fortnight will still give you the space and positive focus for development.

Whether on your own or with other people, it is useful to begin with some appropriate daily declarations and a guided meditation. For clairvoyant development it will help if you choose meditations with a strong visual component. The more that you can visualize and practise using your inner vision, the clearer that vision will be for receiving clairvoyant information. If you have particular religious or spiritual beliefs you may also like to begin with a favourite prayer or invocation. As an example, here is an invocation of positive intent which I have created for clairvoyant development.

INVOCATION – THE CLAIRVOYANTS' PRAYER

I awaken my inner vision with humour, love and positive intent, asking that the clairvoyance I receive is aligned to my highest good, my greatest spiritual development and the highest good of all concerned.

I ask that my mind be illuminated by the light of higher consciousness, so that I may receive information with joy and interpret whatever information I receive with love, clarity, wisdom and compassion.

I ask that my clairvoyant ability blesses other people with comfort, strength, guidance and support, and that my clairvoyance creates only good in the world.

I ask that my clairvoyance be safe and productive and that it is easy for me to open and close my inner eye at the right time and in the appropriate way.

I ask that my clairvoyance, and all my psychic skills, support me in spiritual growth, balance, harmony and success.

I give thanks for the development of my clairvoyant abilities.

So thank you God, Goddess, Universe, Angels, All that is.

CLARIFYING YOUR INTENTION

Daily declarations, positive affirmations, prayers and invocations aid the expansion and use of psychic abilities by clarifying the intention that we have for our general psychic development as well as the purpose we may assign to a specific sitting or meditation. It is useful to send a clear message to our inner senses, our unconscious awareness and our higher mind, and to communicate our intention to any guiding or supporting energies which may be available to us so that we may become more available to the kinds of clairvoyant information that we are willing to receive. Very simply, we are more likely to get what we want, in the way that is most appropriate for us, if we remember to ask. This is important to remember, whether we are focusing specifically on our clairvoyant abilities or working with any of our other psychic senses.

In a group or individual sitting it may be useful to follow up the initial declarations, meditations and prayers with some more specific questions, statements and requests. For example:

- 'I now wish to receive some guidance from my higher awareness.'

- 'I am now available for clairvoyant information from spirit guides and helpers.'

- 'I am now available for telepathic information from the higher mind of friends and clients who seek my help and support.'

- 'I would like some guidance to help me to improve my relationship with my son.'

- 'What can I best do to aid my spiritual development at this time?'

- 'How can I safely expand and develop my clairvoyance further?'

- 'What do I most need to know or learn about myself right now?'

This next exercise will help you to clarify your intent before you begin a meditation or sitting, and will give you some specifics to refer to as you progress beyond your preliminary visualizations and declarations.

Exercise: Creating a Plan of Intent

With a pen and paper, instinctively answer the following questions and make notes to which you can refer during your next meditation or sitting.

- *Which psychic abilities would I particularly like to develop during this session?*
  For example: clairvoyance, clairaudience, clairsentience, telepathy, auric sight, channelling abilities, automatic writing, etc. (refer to the other areas of this book for more information about specific abilities).

- *From where would I like to receive psychic information and guidance?*
  For example: your own higher mind or higher awareness, spirit guides and helpers, the higher mind of friends/family/ clients, etc., friends or family in spirit, the group mind or collective consciousness, the higher universal intelligence within all things, etc.

- *What would I like to receive information about?*
  For example: you may need help and guidance with specific health or emotional problems, you may need to make some appropriate choices regarding your career or relationships, or you may wish to receive some information for the support, guidance and healing of another person.

- *How would I like to develop spiritually during this session?*
  For example: you may benefit from receiving guidance about
  particular spiritual practices or aspects of personal development which would benefit your growth at this time. You may
  wish to clarify that the choices you are currently making are
  in line with your greater spiritual purpose and development.

Remember to ask for visual information from your higher
self which relates to what you need to know or learn about
yourself right now. If you utilize your process of psychic
development to support your spiritual growth and personal
development, then the process is likely to be happier, healthier and more fulfilling for you.

Having created your plan of intent, you will benefit from keeping your notes at hand and referring to them to state your
requests and ask specific questions during any sittings or
meditations you may embark upon. However, it is possible that
you will not always use them because your higher self and guiding energies will have already tuned in to your needs during
your process of clarification.

Of course, not all clairvoyant sittings and psychic work need
to be so structured. People with developed psychic senses will
often receive and work with information at any time of the day
or night; nevertheless it is useful to have a level of clarity and
regularity when you are first starting out. Even experienced psychics may still choose to operate by sitting regularly and clarifying their intention because it can be useful in strengthening
their abilities further and in setting up clear work patterns and
boundaries.

Let us proceed towards a time when you are a developed, experienced and able clairvoyant, with some more daily declarations, meditations and exercises.

DAILY DECLARATIONS FOR GREATER CLAIRVOYANT VISION

- I AM AVAILABLE FOR HIGHER CLAIRVOYANT INFORMATION.

- MY VISION BECOMES BRIGHTER AND CLEARER EVERY DAY.

- IT IS SAFE AND EASY FOR ME TO BECOME A TALENTED CLAIRVOYANT.

- I TRUST MY HIGHER VISION.

- I SEE MY HIGHEST GOOD WHEREVER I TURN.

One way to strengthen and safely accelerate our development in any area is to imagine ourselves to be fully competent, confident and skilled from the outset. This is useful in mastering any new skill, such as learning to paint, draw, ski or ride a bicycle; psychic ability is no different in this respect. The meditation that follows allows you to visualize yourself as a fully developed clairvoyant and then to access that positive, future vision to stimulate your current growth and development.

Meditation: Becoming a Seer

- Once again, find somewhere quiet and comfortable to sit. Sit or lie down with your back supported and your body open and relaxed, your arms and legs uncrossed.

- Visualize yourself at some future time in your life when you have become a fully evolved and developed clairvoyant. You are able to receive impressively clear, detailed and valuable information to help your own growth as well as the growth and development of others. Your ability to see clearly and interpret what you see with wisdom, humour and compassion is inspirational for everyone who comes into contact with you. On a personal level, your advanced clairvoyant abilities have brought you joy, stability and peace of mind. The information that you receive keeps you eternally youthful while constantly adding to your spiritual maturity.

- In your mind's eye, imagine what you would look like as a developed clairvoyant. Do you dress differently or are you wearing similar clothes to the ones that you have generally worn in the past? What does your hair look like? What mood is conveyed through your face, eyes and posture? How do you use your clairvoyance? What purpose does it serve for you? Paint this picture of your future self as vividly as you can.

- Next, ask your future self for any messages of guidance and inspiration that will support you in your spiritual and psychic development right now. Notice any visual images, thoughts, feelings or impressions that you receive. Ask if there is anything that you need to do to harness your psychic potential at this time. Regardless of whether or not you receive any specific information, thank your future self for her or his support.

- Finally, imagine that your future self sends a beam of bright light from the future back to touch you in the present. See the light penetrate your third eye to stimulate your clairvoyant vision and imagine yourself growing to look, sound and feel like your vision of your future self. Be aware that you already embody the qualities and gifts of the future.

- To complete this meditation, you may wish to visualize a protective curtain of white or indigo blue light around your third eye.

During a sitting, follow up your initial meditations and declarations of intent with the following exercise. It is designed to help you develop greater sensitivity and clarity of focus.

Exercise: Letting in the Light

- Imagine your third eye, at the centre of your forehead, to be like the front lens of a telescope, with the back lens being at a central point between the base of your skull and the nape of your neck. Picture the front and back lenses adjusting in relation to each other so that you have a clear, focused image. This is similar to finding the correct focus for a telescope, a camera or a pair of binoculars.

- When you have finished your adjustments, visualize a bright laser beam of light passing through your mind from the front lens to the back lens. Imagine that this laser light illuminates the areas immediately in front of you and immediately behind you. Next, imagine that you can adjust the depth, field of vision and quality of this light to stimulate your clairvoyant vision in different ways.

- First, have the beam minutely focused for the micro-probing of information. Imagine yourself with the ability to receive detailed clairvoyant messages and with the observational powers of a master detective.

- Then, adjust the beam a little wider so that it can heal and transform everything it touches. Imagine that your vision has a positive influence on the world around you, whether or not you are actively using it.

- Finally, expand the beam even wider to give you an overview of your life, personal development, spiritual purpose and goals. Imagine that you are easily able to take a clear overview of any given situation; be aware of any inspirational images that you receive.

- When you complete your sitting, close your third eye or place the white or indigo light of protection around it in the manner previously described.

INTERPRETING SYMBOLS

Many clairvoyants receive psychic information in full or in part, in the form of symbols and abstract images. For instance, when receiving clairvoyant information for someone who is looking for guidance to help deal with persistent ill-health and nagging minor symptoms, one might receive a clairvoyant symbol of a plant that is wilting and unable to flower. As one continues to look at this image, the emphasis is drawn to the roots of the plant, which are unable to draw sustenance from the dry, infertile, stony ground that they are placed in. One way of interpreting this symbol would be to ask this person about her or his home environment. It could be that this person's physical or emotional surroundings are unsuitable and that a move to a more sustaining, nurturing place would be beneficial. Another interpretation of this symbol may be that this person is not eating correctly and that a change of diet could be in order.

As you can see, this kind of clairvoyant work is quite subjective both in its perception of the initial image and in the interpretation of it. However, clairvoyants who are practised and experienced at this can be incredibly accurate in their interpretations, and these abstract images can prove to be very powerful tools for counselling and guidance. When working with other people in this way it can sometimes be useful to describe the symbol that you are receiving and find out if it makes sense to them. Often, the person her- or himself will know what the underlying message is about, even if you are unsure of the interpretation. However, as with all psychic guidance and counselling it is valuable to remain sensitive to the needs of the other person and adjust the level of interpretation accordingly. Some people are better able than others to handle the information that they are given; in some cases it might be better not to discuss the symbol you receive, sticking instead to a very tactful interpretation. Careful observation of others and the gradual development of your personal style will help you in this.

Depending upon the kind of psychic work you are best suited for, you could receive clairvoyant images that relate to past lives, telepathic communication, underlying life goals or life purpose, aspects of healing and overall spiritual development as well as an individual's current relationships, life choices and career path. Indeed, the range of information that you could receive is too wide for me to categorize effectively. Interpretation is something to be learned over time and is not something that can be easily taught. There is no clairvoyant symbol that has a set meaning or which can be interpreted using a standard formula. Ultimately we all need to trust ourselves, risk making mistakes and practise as much as we can. If you do not understand the clairvoyant messages that you receive, then remember to ask for more information. Your higher awareness and spirit guides will usually do their best to help you. In the meantime, here are some daily declarations to support you.

DAILY DECLARATIONS FOR EFFECTIVE INTERPRETATION

- IT IS EASY FOR ME TO INTERPRET THE CLAIRVOYANT SYMBOLS AND IMAGES THAT I RECEIVE.

- I AM ALWAYS GIVEN THE INFORMATION THAT I CAN BEST UNDERSTAND.

- MY POWERS OF INTERPRETATION ARE SUBTLE AND EFFECTIVE.

- I INTERPRET EVERYTHING THAT I SEE WITH CARE AND COMPASSION.

- MY VISION IS BLESSED WITH WISDOM, IMAGINATION AND CLEAR UNDERSTANDING.

OBJECTIVE CLAIRVOYANCE

Objective clairvoyant ability tends to be more unusual than the subjective kind, but there are still many people who have potential within this area, just waiting to be developed. An objective clairvoyant will see objects, animals or people in spirit as if they were physically present. Unlike subjective clairvoyants, who may get a clear picture of similar subjects internally, objective clairvoyants see things in the environment around them. In some cases these images can be as three-dimensional as a familiar armchair, although the quality of depth, colour and solidity may vary. The experience is more akin to looking at things through our physical vision rather than through our third eye. However, a level of heightened activity in the brow chakra is usually involved.

My own personal experiences of objective clairvoyance have been minimal. For a period of about a year I used to catch a glimpse of a cat out of the corner of my eye, only to discover that there was nothing more tangible to see once I had turned around to get a better look. Indeed, I have had fleeting glimpses of a number of things and people in this way, only to have full objective clairvoyant vision elude me when I have looked closer. Many of us have experiences like this and put it down to our imagination or just a trick of the light, but I have heard plenty of first-hand accounts from people who do have objective vision to be reasonably convinced of the validity of these experiences and this particular kind of clairvoyance.

A number of men and women that I have spoken to over the years have described being visited by people in spirit or of witnessing scenes from the past. In a number of instances they have seen members of their family or friends who have died some time previously, and I have heard reports of active conversations where people have been able to resolve unfinished business between themselves and/or a third party and the person in spirit. Indeed, both objective and subjective clairvoyants may choose to be involved in an activity that is often described as 'rescue work', where they elect to help people in spirit to come to an understanding of their position, let go of the world of matter and move on spiritually. This is usually a gentle process of healing and negotiation that is often best done as a group activity with an experienced teacher.

In more than one case, the people sharing their experiences of objective clairvoyance with me had not previously considered themselves to be psychic and would not necessarily have told other members of their family for fear of not being believed. Similar to people with other psychic abilities, the majority of objective clairvoyants I have spoken to have been ordinary people who do not make a fuss about the things that they see. Certainly, I have heard many stories of this nature from people who would be generally considered to be sensible, rational and down-to-earth.

Some objective clairvoyants tend to see spirit guides and helpers rather than family or friends in spirit. There are count-less reports of people who see beings that they describe as angels, hovering around them during times of illness, crisis or great emotional need. Visions of guides, helpers and angels, whether objective or subjective, can bring great reassurance to both the psychics themselves and to anyone with whom they are working. Visions of this nature may be linked to messages of encouragement or wisdom that are transmitted through subjec-tive clairvoyance, clairaudience or direct channelling.

If you are already naturally attuned to objective vision then you may need to concentrate simply upon defining the parameters of what you are willing to see and work with. This you can do by creating an appropriate plan of intent similar to the one outlined earlier in this chapter (*see page 64*). If you have the potential to develop objective clairvoyance but have yet to discover it, then all of the exercises for subjective clairvoyance will help you to develop your visual acuity; other exercises within this book will help you to strengthen and broaden your psychic range. With regular practice, objective ability will follow. For now, you could make a start with the following declarations.

DAILY DECLARATIONS
FOR OBJECTIVE VISION

* IT IS SAFE FOR ME TO BE AN OBJECTIVE CLAIRVOYANT.

* I AM WILLING TO DEVELOP TANGIBLE CLAIRVOYANT VISION.

* MY VISION IS FILLED WITH OBJECTIVITY, SOLIDITY, DEPTH
  AND COLOUR.

* I SAFELY STIMULATE MY OBJECTIVE CLAIRVOYANT
  POTENTIAL.

* IT IS EASY FOR ME TO RECOGNIZE OBJECTIVE CLAIRVOYANT
  IMAGES.

AURIC SIGHT

Strictly speaking, auric sight is not a type of clairvoyance, although when we take the term clairvoyance literally it needs to be acknowledged that the ability to see auras is certainly a form of clear vision. However, auric sight is quite different in nature to the clairvoyant abilities that I have described above.

Auric sight is the ability to see the subtle energetic field or 'aura' that emanates from all physical things. While we may think of auric fields in relation to human beings, it is important to note that everything has an aura: mammals, birds, fish and all forms of animal life; trees, flowers and all forms of plant life; stones, rocks and other supposedly inanimate objects. Whatever you can think of will have its own subtle energetic body that can be seen, felt and observed. Even your favourite piece of furniture has an aura!

An aura may look like a photographic double image or an 'electrical' cocoon around the person, life-form or object in question. Sometimes the aura of a human being quite tightly follows the lines and curves of the physical body; at other times it is much more expanded. It can be proportionally larger or smaller in particular areas depending upon an individual person's state of health, energy levels, mood, thought patterns and underlying spiritual purpose.

Auras can vary in texture, quality, feel and colour in relation to the vibrational nature of each individual. We all have a basic vibrational rate that fluctuates from moment to moment as we change and develop.

DAILY DECLARATIONS FOR
AURIC VISION

- IT IS SAFE FOR ME TO SEE AURAS

- I EASILY SEE AND PERCEIVE FULL-COLOURED AURAS.

- I DEVELOP A POWERFUL HEALING RELATIONSHIP WITH
  LIGHT AND COLOUR.

- I EFFECTIVELY AND SENSITIVELY INTERPRET THE COLOUR,
  DENSITY AND QUALITY OF AURAS.

- MY AURIC VISION BRINGS THE BENEFIT OF HEALING FOR
  MYSELF AND OTHERS.

Exercise: Picturing the Aura

- As before, find somewhere quiet and comfortable to sit. Sit or lie down with your back supported and your body open and relaxed, your arms and legs uncrossed.

- Close your eyes and imagine that you can see an aura around everything. Start with yourself. What might your aura look like at the moment? What colour do you imagine it to be? Is it bright or muted? How big is it? Is it drawn in fairly close to your body or is it quite large and expanded? Trust your instincts; depending upon how visual you are you may get mental pictures of your aura or you may paint the picture with ideas, concepts, feelings or sensations. Trust your mind to do this in whatever way is natural for you.

- Next, open your eyes for a moment and look at an object that is physically close to you. Close your eyes again and imagine its aura. What does it look like? What does it feel like? How is the aura of this object different from your own?

• Finally, open your eyes and take a few moments to look more widely at your surroundings. Close your eyes again and imagine that everything around you has an aura. Focus in on specific objects or perhaps a particular plant or a pet and visualize the kind of aura that each object of your focus may have. Trust your inner vision to give you interesting information and make a note of anything that you perceive or imagine. Complete this exercise by opening your eyes and taking a good look around you once again.

Often, beginning to develop auric sight is a matter of simply learning how to re-focus your eyes. Normally our eyes are focused upon the physical nature of solid matter rather than the subtle energetic field within or around it.

Exercise: Re-focusing Your Eyes

• To begin, comfortably hold up one hand a short distance (about 2 ft/50 cm) from your eyes. Look at your hand, noticing the lines, shapes and texture of the skin. Notice the outline of your fingers and thumb as you gently stretch and contract your hand.

• Next, leave your fingers loosely apart from one another and then consciously shift your focus from your hand to something in the distance. For instance, if you are indoors you may look beyond your hand to a picture upon the far wall of the room you are sitting in. Allow your hand to remain central to your field of vision but look through it or beyond it towards your distant focus. Practise shifting your vision back and forth a few times between your hand close to you and your chosen object further away. Notice how different your hand looks as you adjust your focus back and forth.

- Rest your eyes for a moment and then repeat this process. This time leave your eyes focused in the distance, through or beyond your hand, for a while and notice what you see. Some people may notice a small movement of light or energy around the hand, others may see a double-image etched in white or blue-grey. If you are particularly attuned to auric vision you may see your hand bathed in a field of coloured light.

- It does not matter if you see nothing or very little on your first attempts. Just rest your eyes and have another go later. It is enough that you begin to exercise or stretch your vision in this direction. Often it will be easier for you to use your auric vision at certain times of the day. I generally find the soft light of evening particularly good for developing auric ability.

Exercise: The Aura of Life

- Using the same principles outlined in the exercise above, practise looking at the living things that are around you. You could choose a specific tree, pot plant or sleeping pet to focus upon and then allow your eyes to de-focus or look into the distance in the same manner.

- Before you begin it may also help you to close your eyes and imagine that you are gently contacting the subtle energetic field of the plant or animal in question. With your thoughts, ask permission to proceed and request that the auric body of the life-form involved be revealed to you. If you remember to look at all life with love and respect you are more likely to develop greater awareness and visual acuity.

Exercise: The Human Aura

- With a partner, sit opposite each other at a distance of about 3 or 4 ft (90 cm–1.2 m). Close your eyes for a moment, breathe deeply and imagine that you are gently contacting the subtle energetic field of this person. With your thoughts, ask permission to proceed and request that the auric body of your partner be revealed to you.

- Open your eyes and take a good look at your partner physically first, and then, allowing the focus of your eyes to change, look at the aura. It may help for the two of you to synchronize your breathing by inhaling and exhaling at a similar pace and rhythm. Remember to look through, beyond or around the physical image of your friend to see the subtle electrical field that she or he emanates. Notice any clairsentient, clairvoyant or clairaudient information that you also receive as you do this. You may find that your exploration of auric sight stimulates your other psychic channels.

- When you complete this exercise remember to separate from your partner by imagining a safety curtain of light, sound and feeling unfurling between you.

INTERPRETING THE AURA

If you begin to see coloured auras and wish to interpret what you see, it would be best to start by placing greater emphasis upon the quality of the colour rather than on the colour itself. Ask yourself, *'Is the quality of the aura clear and bright or is it muted or even muddy?', 'What does my intuition tell me about the auric field, does it look strong and well formed or is it wispy, ragged or uneven?', 'Is this the aura of a person who is currently healthy, happy and relaxed or am I receiving different signals?'*

The interpretation of auric colours can never be standardized. We are all individuals and therefore each of us has a unique relationship with colour. As a general guide, however, warmer colours relate to slower-moving vibrational energy, physical well-being and material concerns, while cooler colours relate to faster-moving vibrational energy, spiritual well-being and the higher awareness. Here is a simple guide to the meaning of different colours. Please use it as a starting point for your intuition and not as a hard-and-fast set of rules.

Red *basic survival*
the 'fight or flight' instinct
the building-blocks of life
physical strength and motivation
material concerns
raw power and energy
anger
revolutionary change

Orange *physical vitality*
sensuality
sexuality
pleasure
exercise
creative motivation
warmth
passion

Orange is often a colour associated with sportsmen and -women, dancers and athletes.

Yellow *inspiration*
intellectual activity
the power of the mind
academic study
bright ideas
cheerfulness
the bridge between the mind and
     the body
the higher intelligence of the body

Green *the natural world*
balance
harmony
neutral influences
calmness
regulating energy
love
compassion
ecological awareness
the bridge between the emotions
     and higher reason

Bright blue *communication*
healing
teaching ability
creativity
expression
detachment
inspiration
the impulse to communicate
mass communication

Blue can sometimes be strongly
present in medical environments
or around complementary
therapists.

Indigo blue *vision*
intuition
psychic ability
spiritual protection
the higher functions of the brain
visual acuity
auditory skills
the bridge between the
    hemispheres of the brain

Violet *spiritual growth*
wisdom
the pathway to enlightenment
the bridge between the mind
    and the higher mind
the bridge from the higher mind
    to the collective
    consciousness

Pink *love*
warmth
tenderness
the impulse to nurture
childhood concerns
the safety of the inner child

Gold *love*
brilliance
prosperity
spiritual radiance
higher creativity
the breath of the divine

White *purity*
purification
the higher realms of perception

chapter four

YOUR INNER HEARING

LISTEN – DO YOU WANT
TO KNOW A SECRET?

Most of us are aware of a degree of inner listening. We inwardly hear a constant stream of thoughts spilling out from our subconscious or unconscious mind and into our conscious awareness. This may be less apparent when we are fully engaged in some external activity such as taking part in a passionate debate or when we are bombarded with the noise and chatter of the modern world. However, our stream of thoughts is still there, providing us with a constant inner dialogue of impressions, opinions, judgements and ideas.

Much of our inner chatter is based upon beliefs and attitudes that we have formed in the past. Like sophisticated tape recorders, our minds imprint a memory of our experiences and our response to those same experiences in the form of core beliefs and choices. We develop an extensive library of information that we can refer to for assessing and comprehending future events. It is our ability to do this that helps us to make sense of the world and allows us to learn from our mistakes, but it is also a way in which we may sometimes choose our limitations or pre-judge people and situations without proper consideration of the facts.

I believe, however, that there are other sources of information that we can access from within. There are areas of knowledge and awareness which, when combined creatively with our 'tapes' of belief and past experience, allow us to think in more inspirational, original ways. When we listen to and act upon these areas of information they can help us to take new approaches to our lives, be particularly inventive and grow towards a state that many spiritual teachers have referred to as enlightenment.

We all have the ability to access these more enlightened thoughts but some of us are more naturally attuned to the frequencies that they are broadcast on. However, the art of tuning in can be developed with practice.

TUNING IN TO CLAIRAUDIENCE

Have you ever heard someone speaking to you only to turn around and realize that there is no one physically present? Like clairvoyance, some clairaudient ability is quite objective in nature. Objective clairaudients hear psychically transmitted sounds and spoken language as if they were hearing them physically. Indeed, the rare clairaudients with this ability sometimes question their sanity when they first encounter this phenomena. What they hear may not be too dissimilar to the normal sounds of daily life, yet the source may not be immediately apparent.

Most of us, however, are more likely to develop subjective clairaudience. The psychic noises we hear are received as impressions of sounds or words or, alternatively, thoughts, concepts and ideas that just seem to appear in our minds.

Some people receive their best ideas from clairaudient messages. Solutions to problems, business strategies, new inventions and personal guidance may all be transmitted through clairaudience as well as some of the other psychic senses I have discussed. We may psychically 'hear' words of reassurance or sounds that brighten our mood and help to heal us from depression. Our clairaudience may support us when we are facing powerful life choices, offering options we may not previously have considered or confirmation that we are on the right path.

Perhaps even more than some other psychic abilities, clairaudience is often a case of 'tuning in' to the right frequencies. Physical sound is said to vibrate at particular rates, and the same is true for clairaudient sound. The key is to widen the range in which we are able to receive and perceive information through the hearing senses so that we are able to discern sound resonance that is outside the confines of our physical sense of hearing. Here are some declarations and exercises to help us begin.

DAILY DECLARATIONS FOR CLAIRAUDIENCE

* I SAFELY EXPAND THE RANGE OF MY HEARING.

* MY HEARING BRINGS ME JOY AND TRANSFORMATION.

* I OPEN MY EARS TO THE SOUNDS OF LOVE AND LAUGHTER.

* IT IS SAFE FOR ME TO DEVELOP MY CLAIRAUDIENCE.

* MY EARS ARE SAFELY ATTUNED TO HIGHER FREQUENCIES.

Exercise: Tuning the Radio

Sit comfortably with your back supported and your body open and relaxed, your arms and legs uncrossed. Breathe deeply and, with your thoughts, place a shield of golden light around your ears for healing and protection. Imagine that the light is filled with a steady, high-pitched sound, a little like a continuous chime that creates a sense of peace, balance and clarity within you. Know that as you expand your range of hearing you automatically tune in to frequencies that are safe and beneficial for you at this time. The light and its corresponding chime make you magnetic to the sounds of love, joy and inspiration. All information you receive is in line with your highest good.

Next, imagine yourself with an inner dial like a radio and a knob that you can turn to tune your hearing in to the following frequencies:

1] Your own higher self. Imagine that you are able to tune your hearing in to the frequencies of your own higher awareness. This is the part of you that sees the bigger picture of your life, even when your conscious mind is in a state of confusion. The higher awareness often acts as a bridge for a range of psychic information that originates from outside sources, so it is always a good place to start. What is more, the higher mind when listened to can help us to filter out any information or experiences that are not appropriate for us. You could represent this 'tuning in' to yourself by imagining a subtle change in sound or picturing yourself entering a specific area of your dial.

2] The realms of your higher guides. Hold an intention that you wish to connect only to the realms of higher guidance and ask that you work with guiding energies which truly serve your highest good. Once you have sent out this clear mental message, imagine tuning your hearing to receive clairaudient information from your higher guides. Sense a subtle sound change as before and see yourself moving into another area of your dial.

3] Areas of the natural world. Imagine tuning your hearing so that you are available to the subtle sound vibrations of the natural world. The spirits of animals and plants have their subtle sounds and you may have a special ability to work with nature. Some people can even 'hear' as well as feel changes in the weather before they occur.

In all cases, note any information that comes to you through your ears, your other psychic senses or your imagination. Make a note of any insights you have. You may receive very little clairaudience when you first practise this, but it is worth persisting. After a while you may find that your ears automatically tune in to receive clairaudient information at particular times and in appropriate situations.

Complete this process by bringing your hearing safely back to the frequencies of your own higher awareness and by shielding your ears once again with protective light and sound. Avoid practising this exercise immediately before you spend time in very busy, noisy places.

Exercise: Listening to Guidance

When you have practised 'tuning in' a few times on different occasions you may wish to listen for some specific aspects of guidance. Begin by taking a few minutes to write down some questions or areas of enquiry that are important for you at this time and then 'tune in' in the normal way. Slowly ask your questions and take some time to breathe deeply and listen for responses. Remember to make a note of any insights you receive, and make sure you 'tune out' and protect your hearing once you are complete. Here are some examples of questions you could ask:

'What can I best do at this time to strengthen and enhance my psychic abilities?'

'What can I do to heal my life?'

'How can I best use my psychic gifts?'

In addition, you may wish to ask questions about the source of the information that is coming to you. Whose voice, concept or idea are you listening to? Notice any clairvoyant or clairsentient information that you may also receive.

WORDS AND MESSAGES FROM
THE HIGHER MIND

Most of us certainly receive a degree of clairaudient information from our higher mind. Usually we are unaware of it because it has always been there. Clairaudient words of wisdom may just seem like common sense from a familiar inner voice and, indeed, that is often exactly what it is. We all receive a constant stream of information from our own higher awareness, and a certain amount of that information is clairaudient or auditory in nature. We just need to remember to listen. Sometimes I hear names repeated over and over in my mind, the names of people I already know or of people I am being encouraged to meet and get to know better.

Towards the end of 1991, my partner Justin Carson and I were scheduled to lead one of our regular courses in self- healing techniques. We had handled the booking of this course ourselves and were already a little familiar with the names of our participants, even though we had not previously met any of them. For no apparent reason two names stuck in my mind: 'Caroline' and 'Lena'. For some days before the course I would close my eyes to sleep at night and hear a voice inside my head, constantly repeating these names. During the daytime when I was engaged in tasks that did not command my full concentration, the voice would come again, clearly repeating these women's names but not giving me any other discernible information. I just took it as a sign that I needed to pay particular attention to these two people who were booked to attend the course.

Caroline and Lena turned out to be particularly remarkable and lovable women who run a charity for people with special needs called The Caring and Sharing Trust. Their activities include extraordinary healing work with music, visual arts and live performance. They quickly became very good friends of ours, and although we do not see each other very often, we were able to support each other through a particularly challenging period of our lives.

Experiences like this are very common. The higher mind or higher awareness gives us many clues or pointers to the life choices we need to make and to the people we need to meet and learn from along the way. The way that our higher mind communicates to us will depend upon the precise nature of our natural intuitive or psychic abilities, but a significant area of this communication may well be partly clairaudient. We may have words, names or sounds whispered into our ears or particular thoughts or concepts that just seem to arrive in our minds, seemingly from nowhere and sometimes accompanied by interesting sensations around the ears. Many people talk of the therapeutic need to be silent and listen to that still, small voice within. Often that voice is directed or guided by the impulses of the higher mind.

STRENGTHENING YOUR CONNECTION
TO YOUR HIGHER AWARENESS

The more attention we give to our higher mind, the more we strengthen the connection between our normal consciousness and our higher consciousness. Every time we listen to our intuition and take practical steps to act upon the guidance we receive, we enhance our higher awareness. What is more, when we act with a sound degree of honesty, integrity and self-worth, the higher mind delights in supporting us. This part of ourselves has a clearer view of our spiritual development than we have at a conscious level and it is committed to our greatest purpose, joy and success.

Our higher mind is our greatest ally. It is important to consult this part of ourselves when we are making significant changes in our lives, facing important decisions or wishing to take the appropriate step towards greater psychic awareness. Through our own higher mind we can connect to the higher mind of others to negotiate with them, bringing healing to our relationships and success to group projects. The higher mind can communicate in ways that free us from our day-to-day human dramas and align us to our greatest spiritual potential.

DAILY DECLARATIONS FOR HIGHER AWARENESS

- I TRUST MY OWN HIGHER WISDOM.

- IT IS SAFE FOR ME TO MOVE TO THE NEXT LEVEL OF AWARENESS NOW.

- I FULLY CONNECT TO THE GUIDANCE THAT IS AVAILABLE FOR ME.

- I AM WILLING TO RECEIVE HIGHER GUIDANCE.

- I EASILY RECEIVE MESSAGES OF HIGHER WISDOM.

Meditation: Accessing Your Higher Awareness

- Sit comfortably with your back supported and your body open and relaxed, your arms and legs uncrossed. Breathe deeply and, as before, place a shield of golden light and sound around your ears.

- Imagine that your higher mind exists within a beautiful palace of light and sound. The palace is located somewhere above you; to access it you need to find the entrance from within. As you breathe, visualize yourself filled and surrounded by a web of silver lights. Imagine yourself safely climbing up this web, drawn towards the palace entrance by notes of beautiful music that quiver seductively down through the silver threads. As you climb the music sounds brighter, clearer and sweeter, giving you all the energy you need to ease your way upwards.

- Your web of silver brings you to a jewelled gateway that leads onto an extraordinary courtyard. Create a symphony of sound, light, images, concepts and feelings with your imagination to represent this place clearly in your mind. This is the home of your higher intelligence. You are free to spend time here whenever you choose. Notice an endless supply of joyful impulses, inspirational ideas and wisdom whizzing around you in the form of higher sounds, images and sensations. If you reach out your hands you can catch some to take away with you. Take some time to explore the feeling of this place and to listen to the music of your higher awareness.

- When you leave, see yourself bringing some of the images, sounds and sensations of your higher mind back with you to inspire you on the next steps of your life and psychic journey.

Picture yourself climbing down the web of silver until your feet are placed firmly on the ground once again. Each time you repeat this process, you strengthen your connection to your higher mind. Imagine yourself expressing your highest awareness in every waking moment and make a note of any ideas or insights you receive.

WORDS OF WISDOM FROM GUIDES AND HELPERS

Many psychics believe that they are guided by personalities in spirit who are able to offer valuable information and support through clairaudience, clairvoyance, clairsentience and forms of direct channelling. Some believe that their guides are people who were once physically alive and who now inhabit a higher spiritual dimension. In some cases, their guides may be considered to be known relatives, friends or former partners who continue to offer guidance to the people they love beyond the limits of their physical mortality. Others, subscribing to a belief in reincarnation, claim the psychic intervention of spirit guides who take the form of personalities they once knew in a former life.

Many more psychics talk of spirits who are considerably more enlightened than we are and who continue to advance their spiritual growth by assisting us with ours. Western spiritualists have claimed guides who, in life, were born of races and cultures that have much to teach us. I have known of healers, channels and clairvoyants who claim to have Chinese doctors, Tibetan monks, African medicine men, native American shamans and Indian mystics as guides. Some consider their spirit guides to be angels: in my opinion, there is a great deal of anecdotal evidence to suggest that true guides are, at least, partly angelic in nature.

I personally believe in the existence of spirit guides but I also believe that the form in which they appear or speak to us is dependent upon our own spiritual and psychological personalities. It would make sense to me that any truly helpful and enlightened spirit is going to work with us in ways that are congruent with our individual belief system and our special abilities. From my experience, it would appear that most people have not one but a whole team of spirit guides who bring support to various aspects of their lives and spiritual development.

Some individual guides are more involved in our growth at certain times in our lives than at others. If, for example, we are learning particular creative skills, it would make sense to have the appropriate teachers available to us at that time. If, a few years later, the skills we are developing are more to do with the development of our psychic potential, then it would be appropriate to have contact with guides who are equipped to help us develop in this area.

I do not think that all spirits are spirit guides. I believe that there are a number of trapped souls who have not learned to let go of their attachment to the world of matter and who therefore linger around people or places they once knew. Contrary to popular fiction, most of these spirits are benign. At most they may be lost and confused. Indeed, there are some psychics who choose to become involved in what is commonly known as 'rescue work' by encouraging these spirits to let go of their earthly attachments and journey towards the higher spiritual dimensions where they can continue to grow and evolve. Work of this kind generally takes training and group support, but some people find it very rewarding.

These lost spirits are what we often describe as ghosts. Very few are mischievous or malicious, and those that appear to be are often just wishing to attract some attention to their predicament. In the normal course of events I believe that most of us have very good spiritual and psychic defences that protect us from harmful influences. These defences include the influence of our true spirit guides, the wisdom of our higher intelligence and the natural survival mechanisms that we are born with. However, if you are ever unsure of the validity of the guidance you are receiving or you suspect that the spirit at the source of the information may have a disruptive intent, you can simply ask for it to leave and be replaced by a higher authority.

Always ask for the highest guidance available to you and do not settle for anything less than loving, considerate, compassionate and balanced psychic information. True spirit guides and angels have our best interests at heart. They come to us with positive intent, good humour, warmth and a genuine concern for our spiritual development.

Meditation: Meeting Your Guides

- Sit comfortably with your back supported and your body open and relaxed, your arms and legs uncrossed. Breathe deeply and, as before, place a shield of golden light and sound around your ears.

- Once again, tune your hearing to the frequencies of your higher mind and imagine yourself climbing up the web of silver light to the palace of your higher awareness. (If you wish to use different images or concepts to represent your connection to your higher intelligence, then please do so.) Trust your intuition to guide you gently to the realms and guidance of your higher mind.

- Once connected to your higher mind, ask for contact with your higher guides. State that you are only available for the highest guidance from sources that have your best interests at heart, and imagine that your hearing, vision and gut sense become attuned to the appropriate frequencies. You become perfectly available to receive higher inspiration and support.

- If you wish to follow my images, visualize your palace of light and sound filled with visiting angels. Some of them may appear to you as beings of pure light, sound or warmth while others may take human form or the shapes of animals, plants or crystals. Trust your imagination to create the ideal concept or paint the perfect picture and notice what you see, hear and feel.

- Visualize a small number of your many guides approaching you and bathing you with feelings of love and acceptance. Notice what they look, feel and sound like and ask them for any guidance they have for you at this time. Stay open-minded to their responses, which may come to you as words of wisdom and common sense or in one of a number of different ways.

- Picture yourself and your guides tuning your inner ears, eyes and senses to different frequencies to find those that are right for you at this time. As an exercise, you could imagine your-self being able to hear the ringing of a Tibetan monastery bell rung by a member of an exiled Tibetan order. Or, alternatively, imagine yourself hearing the vibrations of the oceans and the collective wisdom of the whales and dolphins as they sing messages of peace and enlightenment to you. Feel these creatures connecting to you with love and, in your mind, send back a high vibrational sound of love to them.

- When you have finished exploring these images and sensations, thank your guides for their love and invite them to continue supporting you with their wisdom and good humour. Ask to be always connected to higher guidance and protected from unwanted influences. Gently bring your attention back from your guides and the realm of your higher mind to the physical sensations of your body and the environment around you. See yourself climbing down the web of silver light and placing your feet firmly on the ground beneath you.

- When you complete this meditation, make a note of any insights, ideas, images or feelings you have received.

THE USES OF TELEPATHY

Telepathy is an exchange of information directly from the mind of one individual to the mind of another without the need for words to be spoken aloud or any exchange of physical, non-verbal communication such as eye signals, hand gestures or other forms of body language. However, in the normal course of events telepathy between two human beings who are in close geographical contact with one another is usually combined with all of the above, which is why we rarely notice that we are communicating in this way.

Compatible couples often begin their relationship with the potential to communicate with each other on a similar telepathic frequency, and usually develop a strong sense of telepathy as their relationship evolves and matures. The daily routine of compatible couples will include a level of teamwork and the negotiation of each other's needs based upon a combination of verbal communication, body language and telepathy. There are many instances when the two 'halves' of a couple will have the same thought at exactly the same time, or when one will come up with a new idea that the other voices before the first has a chance to. Part of this is based upon learning, experienced interpretation of each other's signals and a response to similar stimuli, but there is always an element of synchronous thought that is derived from telepathic communication.

Many of us have had conscious experiences of distant telepathy. The simplest example of this is when we find ourselves thinking about another person just a few seconds before that person telephones us. Telepathy seems to be able to work across great distances. It is as common to communicate with a friend who lives on the other side of the world as it is to communicate with someone who lives on the other side of town.

However, the nature of the communication may be different as similarity of environment, experience and thought will influence the frequency upon which we transmit or receive information.

Natural telepathy often exists between a parent and child and is perhaps an integral part of the survival mechanism for babies and young children. The younger and more helpless they are, the more babies need to broadcast their requirements and their whereabouts to anyone who has a biological or emotional investment in their survival – and, of course, their own parents normally come top of the list. The telepathic connection between mother and child can be particularly strong and can continue into the adult life of the offspring. This is no doubt linked to the fundamental physical connection that a baby has with her or his mother throughout the period of gestation and, in many cases, within the first few months of life after birth.

Many professional psychics draw upon telepathic communication more than they often acknowledge. Every human being is an information system: information within us guides our cellular growth, emotional responses and life choices. Memories of past relationships and experiences remain with us even if we lose the ability to recall them, but we may still subtly transmit them to others. Future dreams and aspirations too exist as mental, emotional and spiritual information that can be transmitted and read by gifted psychics.

Good telepathic communication, when combined with good physical and verbal communication skills, can assist relationships to be harmonious. Very few people are so telepathically developed that they can read another person's mind as easily as picking up a book or playing a tape recording but, at the very least, most of us can develop a telepathic sense of mood and timing. A degree of sensitive telepathy can help to make life a little more peaceful, empathic and compassionate. Here are some declarations to help.

DAILY DECLARATIONS FOR TELEPATHY

- I AM WILLING TO RECEIVE SAFE AND POSITIVE TELEPATHIC MESSAGES.

- THE TELEPATHIC CENTRES OF MY MIND ARE FULLY ATTUNED TO HIGHER FREQUENCIES.

- I AM WILLING TO SEND TELEPATHIC MESSAGES OF LOVE, POSITIVITY AND ACCEPTANCE.

- IT IS SAFE FOR ME TO BE FULLY TELEPATHIC.

- IT IS EASY FOR ME TO AWAKEN MY INNATE TELEPATHIC ABILITIES.

CLAIRAUDIENT READINGS FOR OTHER PEOPLE

Once we have practised tuning in to our clairaudience for our own guidance, it may be helpful to begin practising with another person who is also wishing to develop clairaudient ability. As with other psychic work, it is important to respect each other's confidentiality and agree to honour each other's psychic or emotional secrets. You would also benefit from gaining a level of mutual trust that allows you both to risk making mistakes without fear of judgement or criticism. The process of learning needs to feel safe and supportive for all concerned.

The psychic communication you cultivate between yourself and your development partner may emanate from a number of different sources. You may simply generate a good telepathic link or you may receive information from your own higher mind, the higher awareness of your partner, your guides, your partner's guides or a combination of any of the above. While it is important that you negotiate to establish your own way of working together, here are some guidelines to help you.

Exercise: Working with a Partner

- Find a quiet, comfortable spot for you both to sit in. Keep your bodies open, your backs well supported and your arms and legs uncrossed. Sit, either directly opposite your partner or partially opposite one another in a position that allows you a degree of eye contact. If possible it is best to sit fairly close to each other so that you can each give your full attention to the other person.

- Take a few moments to discuss your joint intention. What do you and your partner wish to achieve from this sitting? How would you like your clairaudient abilities to develop? What kinds of information would you like to hear? How long do you intend to sit for? Are you going to take it in turns to read for each other or are you going to respond spontaneously to any information that either of you is given?

- Once you have clarified the purpose of the sitting, close your eyes and start with some deep breathing. Imagine yourself tuning in to your higher awareness and, through your higher mind, imagine that you connect to the higher awareness of your partner. Let your own inner thoughts automatically guide your hearing to expand in the correct way for your needs at this time, tuning in to any relevant guidance for yourself or your partner.

- Imagine that your expanded sense of hearing can pick up your partner's higher self telling you things that would bene-fit you both, and then imagine both your partner's spirit guides and your own guides passing on relevant information. Tell your partner about any insights you hear or receive. After a while, swap over if appropriate. When you complete this exercise, remember to separate from your partner by imagining a safety curtain of light, sound and feeling unfurling between you.

chapter five

YOUR HEALING POTENTIAL

EVERYONE CAN HEAL

Just as I firmly believe that we all have our own unique psychic potential, I also believe that we are all able to develop healing skills for the benefit of ourselves and others. The ability to give hands-on healing, in particular, is a natural human gift. Like any other skill from good physical co-ordination to mathematical ability and from business acumen to being a successful and loving parent, hands-on healing can be stimulated and nurtured. As with any 'gift' there are some people who are more naturally talented healers than others, but we all have the potential to develop. Most of us can at least attain a basic level of competence as a healer. It just takes practice, commitment and a willingness to learn.

WHAT IS A HEALER?

In the widest sense, a healer is a person who creates the space for other people to heal themselves. I believe that we are each responsible for our own self-healing. We may be assisted in the process of healing by doctors, healers, counsellors and complementary therapists, but the miracle of healing is something that occurs inside each of us. Our body, mind, emotions and spirit have their own natural ability to heal and balance themselves when supported to do so.

As a healer, I do not consider that my role is to 'heal' anyone; rather it is to support others in their process of personal development so that healing may occur. Sometimes when I give hands-on healing I imagine the relationship between myself and my client to be quite similar to that of two car engines linked by a set of jump leads. The energy that I channel through my hands, voice, mind and body stimulates the natural healing energy of the recipient, allowing her or his innate physical, mental, emotional and spiritual wisdom to do whatever is needed to re-establish balance and harmony.

Of course, the reality of the relationship between myself and my clients is more sophisticated and much more subtle than the crude illustration above, but it does offer a basic interpretation of the energetic process involved. Being an effective healer also requires a range of counselling skills, a good knowledge of personal development techniques and a practised sensitivity of the subtle energies of the human system. Often, when I am working I can feel exactly where a person's energy is blocked, depleted or over-active and tailor my treatment accordingly. I am also able to support my clients to heal many of the mental, emotional and spiritual states that may be related to the energetic imbalance I have detected. For example, some physical conditions can be related to unexpressed grief. Effective healing may occur with a combination of appropriate physical therapies, hands-on healing and counselling to support the person to handle the grief effectively.

HANDS-ON HEALING

Historically there are many cultural, religious and spiritual traditions that have encouraged the regular use of hands-on healing. Indeed, a number of Christian churches are now rediscovering their healing roots having, in some cases, shunned the practice for the last hundred years or so. Hands-on healing is very old and is one of a number of effective natural healing skills which are currently undergoing a popular revival. Hands-on healing is sometimes referred to as faith healing, spiritual healing and the 'laying on of hands', although all of these terms can be confusing for people who are experiencing healing for the first time.

I tend to use the term 'hands-on' healing because it implies healing through direct human contact and care, although it is not necessary for the healer actually to physically touch clients for healing to occur. Often the hands are used in the healing process, but much of the healing is transmitted through the auric body to the mental, emotional and physical bodies beyond. Some healers may choose to lay on their hands physically, some may not. Both approaches have their advantages. Many people respond very well to physically touch as it helps them to feel comforted and cared for. Most people in the Western world are not touched enough and may associate touch chiefly with sexual contact, so some appropriate touch may be healing in itself. However, working with the hands around only the auric body does reduce the risk of inappropriate physical contact and, for a professional healer, it can help to maintain safe boundaries between healer and client.

The term 'faith healing' is quite confusing because it implies that faith or religious belief needs to be present for healing to occur. The term 'spiritual healing' may also indicate this, although it does give a better assessment of the relationship involved as the energy channelled through the healer to the client can be described as being partly spiritual in nature. It is not essential for the healer or the recipient to have any particular religious or spiritual beliefs. Indeed, the recipient need not have any particular belief in healing at all, just a willingness to participate in the process. From a healer's point of view, it is helpful but not essential to have a client who is open-minded.

To be a healer, it helps to have a belief in the spiritual nature of all things and it is important to be working with a positive, loving intention, but it does not matter whether you are Hindu, Muslim, Christian, Jewish or of any other faith or even if you have no specific religious beliefs at all – healing will still occur.

The hands are simply used in the healing process to guide or direct the flow of healing energy. Using the hands, a healer may focus a greater concentration of healing energy upon a particular part of the recipient's body or towards some inner physical, mental or emotional state. Some people feel warmth in their hands as they heal, some people experience their hands growing colder, while others report a variety of sensations from tingling to a feeling of magnetic attraction or repulsion. All of these sensations indicate that some form of healing energy is present, although experience has taught me that healing often occurs even when the healer feels nothing in her or his hands, nor in any other part of the anatomy. When teaching hands-on healing I have sometimes known inexperienced healers to report feeling very little while their recipients talk enthusiastically about having received tangible sensations of warmth, lightness, peace, release or relaxation.

YOUR HEALING ABILITIES

What healing skills are you already using? You may be surprised by this question and you would not be alone in you surprise. Many people would not think of themselves as natural healers and yet they practise some form of healing on a regular basis. For example, people who have chosen to work in one of a number of caring professions may be unconsciously transmitting healing energy as they administer a range of treatments, listen to the needs of their clients or offer practical guidance and support. Many nurses are natural healers who are unconsciously drawn to their profession because of an underlying desire to heal at more subtle levels.

Numerous counsellors, social workers, chiropodists, health visitors and therapists also unconsciously channel healing energy as well as facilitating some form of healing with the practical skills they possess. Health professionals who already work with their hands, such as masseurs, aromatherapists and reflexologists, generally transmit energetic healing in addition to the physical benefits they provide for their clients. Similarly, people who work in other professions where people are helped to feel or look good are often transmitting healing energy: hairdressers, beauticians, image consultants, make-up artists and exercise trainers would fit into this category.

It could be that you are simply a good, natural listener. I know of people who cannot stand at a bus stop or sit on a train without someone telling them their life story. Often natural healers unconsciously draw people to them who need help, advice or just a sympathetic ear. My mother Lilian is like this. She looks like everyone's favourite Mum or Grandma and she radiates a steady aura of healing energy. However, she does not tend to recognize that she is a natural healer and is not always fully aware of the effect she has on other people.

HOW TO BEGIN

Recognizing the healing abilities that you already possess and use is often the first step to developing new ones. When we acknowledge our unique healing potential we encourage it to grow and we help ourselves to recognize the potential for self-healing within others. No two healers are alike. If you choose to develop your healing abilities you may find that you use similar techniques to other healers but your special gifts will develop from your own personality, interests and insights. People will be drawn to you because of who you are as a person as well as for the healing energy that you channel from beyond you.

The exercises below are intended to help you develop hands-on healing and visual healing skills. Some you can do on your own and some will require you to practise with a partner. Learning the basics of healing is easy. Within my courses, I regularly teach people to give healing in under two hours. Following this introduction, if you wish to become a good professional healer it is important to practise regularly, preferably with a good teacher, and also to consider training in counselling or other healing therapies to help you develop good professional standards of practice.

Let us begin with some daily declarations to stimulate your natural abilities and a meditation to open your special channels of healing.

DAILY DECLARATIONS
FOR HEALING ABILITY

- I EASILY AWAKEN MY NATURAL HEALING ABILITY.

- IT IS SAFE AND EASY FOR ME TO DEVELOP MY HEALING SKILLS.

- I EASILY CHANNEL HEALING LIGHT.

- I TRUST MY NATURAL HEALING WISDOM.

- I CREATE THE SPACE FOR HEALING TO OCCUR.

Meditation: Channelling Healing Light
- Sit comfortably with your back supported and your body open and relaxed, your arms and legs uncrossed. Breathe deeply and notice how your body is feeling. If you are sitting upright, make sure that your feet are planted squarely on the floor in front of you. If you are lying down, be sure to keep your ankles uncrossed.

- Next, take your attention away from your body for a moment and send your thoughts to a special, peaceful place. Imagine that a part of your mind can travel through the depths of space and time to a far distant galaxy some light years away. Within that galaxy there is a beautiful star of golden light energy that exists purely for you. Visualize that golden star. In your mind's eye, look at it from different angles. If you are more inclined to concentrate on feelings, sounds or sensations than visual images, then imagine that this star radiates a gentle warmth, a feeling of loving acceptance and a sound as golden and clear as a beautiful bell. This star contains an unlimited supply of energy for you to use for your own self-healing and for the healing of other people around you. The source of this energy is infinite. It unceasingly brings love and illumination to the darkness of space.

- Picture a beam or column of golden light being projected outwards from the core of your star. See that golden beam grow and extend rapidly, glowing with healing power and potential. Your beam of light extends and travels effortlessly through the depths of space and time. It is magnetic to your thoughts, your body and your special healing gifts. It travels faster than the speed of ordinary light itself, faster than the speed of thought, to enter the earth's atmosphere and extend downwards through the sky in your direction. If you are sitting indoors, see the light passing easily through the roof and the floors of the building you are located within. Imagine your body tingling with anticipation as your column of golden light approaches from above, extending downwards until it is just a few inches above your head.

- Breathe deeply and imagine your healing light passing through your scalp and into your head. Every in-breath helps to draw the light into your body and every out-breath helps the light to brighten and spread into every cell. The light extends down through your head and face, past your shoulders and into the area of your heart and chest. It is here, in your chest, that something even more magical occurs. The light stimulates and strengthens the love from your heart and, in turn, it too becomes stronger and brighter.

- More and more light streams in from above, filling your chest to overflowing. Golden light floods from your heart upwards through your right shoulder, down your right arm, through your wrist and into your right hand where it pulses with healing potential. At the same time the light also floods through your left shoulder, down your left arm and into your left hand.

- See and feel your hands glowing with light, love and healing energy. Lift them gently and rub them together. With your palms flat to each other, imagine the light travelling in a circuit. The energy from your right hand travels onwards into your left and up your left arm to move full circle into your heart and chest. The energy from your left hand is received by the right and also moves full circle up your right arm and back to your heart. Imagine these two circuits of light travelling continually from right to left and from left to right, growing stronger and more brilliant all the time. These circuits of healing power are constantly reinforced by more light that radiates downwards from your column of healing energy above.

- Practise moving your hands away from each other and then back together again. Keep your palms facing each other and imagine that the circuit of light remains strong whether or not your hands are physically touching. Your hands could be far apart and the light would still travel. You may feel a mild electrical charge in your palms or some subtle magnetic repulsion between them as you bring them slowly closer together. Whatever you feel, just notice what is there and continue to play with these ideas and images.

It is valuable to repeat this meditation regularly when you first begin to develop your healing abilities; later on you may choose to do it only occasionally. It acts as a reminder to your body to draw upon the infinite sources of healing energy that exist around you in the universe rather than upon your own physical reserves. If the images do not suit you, or if you sense the energy travelling through you more naturally in a different way, you may wish to adjust the images accordingly. However, there are key points that are worth keeping in mind when you begin to give healing to other people.

SOME KEY POINTS

1] Hold the idea that the healing energy you are channelling is coming from an inexhaustible supply. There are always reserves of healing energy available to you, you just need to keep your thoughts positive and allow yourself to be mentally available for them.

2] Always imagine the energy to be coming from beyond you. The idea is to act as a conduit or channel of healing light rather than as a source of energy yourself. Healers inevitably utilize a certain amount of their own physical, emotional and mental energy when they work, but it is best to use as much 'channelled' energy as possible and to respect your body's own needs. If you regularly become drained when you give healing then it would be a good idea to stop for a while, concentrate upon your own self-healing and practise imagining the energy coming from outside sources.

3] Prepare yourself for healing in a way that is congruent with your own beliefs. If you are profoundly religious you may wish to say a prayer before you begin healing and you may prefer to imagine that the healing light comes directly from God, Jesus, Krishna, Allah or any particular deity or saint. If you hold wider spiritual beliefs you may wish to imagine the light coming from the higher intelligence of the universe, the great spirit, universal love or any other focus you have for spiritual growth and enlightenment. For anyone who holds no particular spiritual beliefs, you may choose to imagine that the healing energy is coming from natural, sustainable sources. Quantum physics theorizes about the subtle but powerful energy that exists within all things. You could visualize the light coming from natural earth energy or atmospheric forces.

4] Whatever your beliefs, healing occurs most effectively when you, as the healer, think positively and constructively about yourself, the process of healing and the healing potential of your clients. Heal with love and respect. If you listen respectfully to other people you will not offer them healing when it is inappropriate. If you listen respectfully to your own needs, you are unlikely to feel burned out or drained after giving healing.

Before you begin to practise healing on others it may be valuable to practise on yourself.

Exercise: Healing Yourself

- Begin with the meditation above and then continue to channel the healing light by placing your hands on or near areas of your body that would benefit from healing at this time. If you cannot reach some areas effectively then place your hands in a comfortable position and imagine the light travelling from them to the appropriate spot.

- For instance, if you have a sore throat and a tight chest, you could place one hand lightly on or near your throat and the other on your chest. You would then imagine the light passing from your hands and into these parts of your body, automatically spreading out to any other areas that need it too. You could picture or sense light, warmth, coolness, relaxation, love or vibrant energy stimulating the whole of your immune system, releasing all tension, discharging any blocked energy, soothing pain, dissolving infection and awakening your body's own natural healing wisdom. Trust your instincts to do whatever is appropriate for you at the time. Remember to trust your intuition, use your imagination and accept that the light will find its way to where it is needed regardless of what you can or cannot currently feel.

- It is important to breathe deeply, and valuable to practise with your hands in different positions. What does it feel like to touch your body physically? How does it feel when your hands are almost touching? Do you receive any particular sensations when your hands are further away? Because we are used to ourselves and our own energetic systems we may find it more challenging to discern movements of energy or fluctuations of feeling within ourselves than when we are working with other people, but it is still valuable to give healing to yourself on a regular basis.

HEALING ANIMALS AND PLANTS

House plants benefit from regular healing, as do pets and other domestic animals. Indeed, there are many excellent healers who specialize in healing pets or farm animals. While I mainly work with people, I have given healing to cats, dogs and horses among others. Like people, animals do not have to be sick to benefit from or enjoy healing, and usually if healing is not appropriate for them they will let you know by dashing off in the opposite direction. Of course, healing is most appropriate when used to support veterinary treatments rather than to replace them. While animals readily respond to natural forms of healing, it is best to consider their overall well-being by getting a good veterinary diagnosis and advice during the earliest stages of illness or injury.

When giving healing to my cats Mitzi and Toulouse, I generally wait until they are comfortably settled upon my lap and then, while stroking or petting them in the normal way, I pause with my hands on or near any area of their body that I instinctively feel would benefit from healing. I avoid any movements that would seem sudden or strange to them and instead generally imagine light being channelled through my hands as I stroke them from head to tail. If an animal is injured, I tend to put my hands near, rather than directly on, the injury. Like humans, animals instinctively defend vulnerable or painful areas and, as healers, we need to work in ways that reduce their anxiety or distress rather than add to it.

If an animal is in particular distress it may even be better to send healing from the other side of the room until the distress has subsided rather than to arouse anxiety that would inhibit the natural healing process. As you send healing, imagine the animal to be healthy and whole. See it returning to full health and use your other psychic abilities to tune in intuitively to specific needs that she or he may have.

To practise healing on plants, have your hands near rather than on the plant in question and imagine its leaves, stem, flowers and roots filling with healing light. You could visualize the plant returning to full health and growing successfully. Remember to take care of the plant by planting, watering, feeding and tending it in the appropriate way.

HEALING PEOPLE

For human beings, as with animals, it is always important to explore a range of medical or complementary therapies that include the use of hands-on healing rather than to focus upon energetic healing alone. I believe that there are many contributory factors to illness – physical, mental, emotional and spiritual – and that the best healing often occurs with a combined approach. Certainly hands-on healing supports the effectiveness of all other treatments and therapies, often reducing the stress of illness and speeding up the recovery rate. Unlike some other therapies, healing is non-invasive and can be used for the prevention of many conditions, the relief of depressive states that often accompany disease and the care of patients who are chronically or terminally ill.

Most people who receive hands-on healing benefit from it in some way, although the actual effect varies from person to person depending upon the skill and experience of the healer, the specific condition being presented for treatment and the personality of the recipient. I consider hands-on healing to be successful if my client becomes more relaxed, more positive and more in control of her or his life and healing process. If in addition there is some marked relief from pain, a reduction of symptoms and an obvious increase in recovery rate then I am delighted. A combination of the above usually occurs, but physical recovery is never my sole purpose for giving healing.

Energetic healing helps people to attain a level of peace within themselves and can often stimulate spiritual growth or psychic awareness. For someone with an ongoing condition, hands-on healing can help in the day-to-day management of symptoms and, for the terminally ill, it can support the peaceful transition from life to death. Healing is not always about physical wellness, sometimes it powerfully assists people to live and die with dignity. As a healer, I help to create a state of grace in which healing can occur.

The healing process that I am about to guide you through is intended as a starting point for your own intuition. Trust your instincts and develop your own style. I do not believe that there is a 'system' of healing that is appropriate for everyone. Indeed, you may soon find yourself simplifying the steps below so that you can give immediate attention to the specific needs of those who come to you for help.

Exercise: Bringing Healing to Others

- If possible, begin practising with a friend or partner who also wishes to develop her (or his) healing abilities. This will allow you to develop your confidence and learn about both sides of the healing relationship, giving and receiving.

- The person receiving healing needs to assume a relaxed, comfortable position: body open, arms and legs uncrossed and, preferably, eyes closed. The latter is certainly not essential but it does help to encourage a state of relaxation. It does not matter whether the recipient is sitting upright or lying down, as long as she is comfortable and can be easily reached from a number of different angles. Make sure that the recipient's back is properly supported and that the room is warm enough. In deep relaxation, body temperature can sometimes drop quite considerably.

- Encourage your 'client' to breathe deeply and relax. If it is appropriate for you both, you could have some soothing music playing in the background. I prefer silence as it makes it easier for me to listen to my intuition and concentrate upon the process in hand, although I often use my voice to guide the person through some visual images or positive thoughts that are intended to complement the healing that is taking place.

- Before you begin, it is often a good idea to discuss the level of physical touch you are intending to use. This allows you to find out whether or not touch is appropriate and what your 'client's' comfort levels are likely to be if you touch particular parts of her body. You can do some very good healing without using any physical touch at all, but your intuition may tell you that some direct contact will be helpful. Negotiate and always give prior warning of when you are going to use touch, so that the other person does not become startled when, for instance, you lay your hands on her shoulders.

Step One

Begin with your hands on or near the head of the recipient. Perhaps start from a few inches (8–10 cm) above, in the region of the crown chakra (*see chakra diagram, page 55*). In your mind, connect to the image (from the meditation, *page 108*) of golden healing light energy travelling to you and through you from your distant star. Imagine your heart filling with light and picture that light flooding out of your body through your hands and into the head of the recipient. Imagine the colour of the light changing until it is the perfect healing shade and vibration for the recipient's needs. Instinctively choose a colour in your mind, or simply make a guess.

Sense the light filling the head, brain and face of the recipient, regenerating, rejuvenating, healing and balancing all physical tissue. At the same time, imagine all tension melting away from the muscles of the head and face. You could picture the light easily and harmlessly dissolving fear, disharmony, tension and disease and, at the same time, stimulating the body's own healing mechanisms. Visualize the recipient healthy and happy, easily and effortlessly developing and using her own healing gifts.

Step Two

Focus upon the eyes, ears, nose and mouth of the recipient. Place your hands on or near the forehead or third eye area and then a few inches (8–10 cm) above the eyes. Imagine the recipient's vision growing stronger, clearer and healthier. Sense the eyes filling with healing light. Do the same with the ears, nose and mouth. Hold your hands a few inches (8–10 cm) away and imagine the light healing the recipient's sense of hearing, smell and taste. Remember to send healing energy to the teeth and gums.

Step Three

Place your hands very lightly on or near the throat and neck of your 'client'. The chakra or energy centre here relates to communication, change, expression and creativity. Imagine the light healing this area on all levels – physical, emotional, mental and spiritual. Imagine this person communicating effectively and making positive, healing changes in her life.

Step Four

Place your hands on or near the recipient's shoulders and imagine all tension or burdens melting away from them. Sense the light soothing the muscles of the shoulders and chest. With your hands, do a few sweeping movements over the person's arms and down towards the hands. Pause at the elbow, wrist or finger joints if you instinctively feel there is a need.

Step Five

Place your hands over the area of the heart and chest. At the top of the chest imagine the light stimulating, healing and balancing the immune system. Lower down, picture the heart and lungs to be in perfect health and gently remind the recipient (if appropriate) to breathe deeply and slowly. Imagine the heart beating with strength and the perfect rhythm for health. Visualize the recipient expanding her capacity to give and receive love as you focus upon the centre of the chest, the heart chakra.

Step Six

Place your hands over the area of the solar plexus, which is located centrally at the base of the ribs and above the stomach. As with the other chakras, this is both a physical area and a subtle energy centre. Imagine the light stimulating, relaxing or balancing this sensitive area. Trust that the energy will do whatever is appropriate. See the light heal the internal organs within this region of the body. It is not important to know the exact positions of organs, the light will go to wherever it is needed.

Step Seven

Focus upon the stomach. Imagine the light healing the digestive system and all the internal organs in this area. The stomach chakra is 2 or 3 inches (5–7.5 cm) below the navel. As well as digestion, assimilation and elimination, this area relates to physical energy, sensuality and sexuality. Imagine the light stimulating the recipient's vitality and motivation.

Step Eight

Place your hands above the groin area and the base of the spine. Because this is such a delicate area it is important to keep your distance and certainly to avoid physical contact, but it is also important to focus plenty of healing light here. The base chakra, located in this region of the body, relates to fundamental issues of life, death and survival. With your mind, send your 'client' thoughts of peace and safety. Imagine her taking on a new lease of life; the healing light safely dissolving all underlying fears and anxieties that this person may have.

Step Nine

Focus upon the spine by placing one hand pointing upwards towards the top of the neck and the other hand pointing downwards towards the base vertebrae. Imagine light pulsing up and down the full length of the spine, healing, regenerating, rejuvenating and relaxing wherever it travels. Depending upon the position of the recipient, this can be done from either the front or the back of the body. Next, do some sweeping passes over the body from the head to the base of the spine. This can be done with one or both hands and at a distance of 2 or 3 ft (60–90 cm) away, according to your preference. As you move your hands, imagine that you are safely dispersing stuck or stale energy, allowing the light to cleanse the whole system.

Step Ten
With your hands, do some sweeping movements down the legs, from the hips to the feet, pausing at the hip, knee and ankle joints if appropriate. Imagine all the joints of the body to be strong and flexible and see the recipient's legs carrying her safely forward in life, guiding this person towards health, harmony and happiness.

Step Eleven
Focus special attention upon the feet. Imagine your recipient becoming more grounded, stable, balanced and practical. Visualize this person able to integrate and utilize all of this healing light to make a tangible difference to her own peace of mind, health and well-being.

Step Twelve
Step back a little to take an overview of this person's body. If there is any area of the body you feel would benefit from additional healing, attend to that now, picturing the light intensifying wherever it is needed. Next, imagine a healing force-field of light around the whole person. The energy of this force-field

keeps the recipient safe and protected, magnetic to any other treatments, therapies, experiences and relationships that would support her healing process at this time.

Once you have completed this process, shake your hands gently to disperse any excess energy and break the connection between yourself and your 'client'. Imagine this person now taken care of by her own self-healing abilities, continuing to heal herself in each new moment.

Gently encourage this person to open her eyes and to bring her attention back to her present environment. Take some time for this, as many people become deeply relaxed and may even be asleep or in a light trance. Sit with the person for a while as she 'comes to' and discuss any feelings or experiences that either of you has had during the healing session. It may be a good idea to give your recipient some pure water to drink to help the body to flush out any toxins.

After healing it is a good idea for both the recipient and the healer to avoid alcohol, tobacco and other recreational drugs for a little while. Many people will become more sensitized to these substances and their effects may seem rather stronger than normal. During my courses I often joke that healing turns us all into cheap dates because a single measure of spirits can have the effect of a triple!

ABSENT HEALING

Absent healing provides us with a simple way to bring help and support to other people without needing to be physically with them or directly involved in their process of healing. Absent work can sometimes be as effective as many forms of healing that involve direct contact between healer and recipient, and does not require any special skills or previous experience. At its simplest, it occurs through a combination of the power of thought and the power of love. Each thought we have is powerful and sends a subtle energetic charge through our own body, through our emotions and out to the world at large. In essence, we are all engaged in telepathic communication at an unconscious level. When we think about someone, that person receives our thoughts even if he (or she) is not consciously aware of it.

Meditation: Sending Absent Healing

- Sit comfortably and close your eyes. Breathe deeply and take a few moments to think about the person you wish to send absent healing to. If you already know this person think about how he looks, the sound of his voice when he speaks and the way that you feel about him. This just helps to anchor him in your mind as you begin to send healing energy. If you do not know this individual personally, it is enough to think of his name for healing to occur, or to ponder other information that you may have about him, such as his circumstances or physical condition.

- Imagine this person surrounded by beautiful healing light. Intuitively choose a colour for this light to be. White or golden light is often helpful, but it is good to trust your first instincts and 'guess' which colour to send. You may also wish to imagine that this light is filled with a beautiful sound or a wonderful feeling to support the recipient in the healing he needs. Imagine the person bathed in light, sound and love; sense him able to use that healing energy in whatever way is appropriate for his needs.

- When this is done as a group activity it is often good for the participants to sit in a circle, comfortably holding hands and imagining that a cocoon of healing light is created by the combined thoughts of everyone present. This cocoon of light is then pictured at the centre of the circle and is fed by a positive energy source that is beyond the group in the spiritual or subtle energetic realms close by. Members of the group can then use their individual thoughts to place friends or family members in the middle of the circle so that they can soak up this healing light. This can be done simply by thinking of someone or by speaking his first name out loud. This method of healing, while a shared activity, is also quite 'hands-off' and discreet. No other information about the recipients needs to be shared.

- Meditations for global healing can be conducted in a similar way, with countries, areas of the world, elements of nature or the entire planet mentally placed in the healing cocoon.

HEALING VISION

A number of people develop a form of healing vision to assist them in their work as counsellors, doctors, nurses, complementary therapists or hands-on healers. Some combine a good ability to see and interpret auric fields with their other diagnostic skills to help them to choose effective treatments or courses of action and to monitor the efficacy of the treatments that their clients are using. At its simplest level, a person who displays a brighter, cleaner, clearer auric field than during a previous consultation is either responding quite well to treatment or improving of her or his own accord. Of course, evidence of this nature is a matter of subjective interpretation and needs to be taken into context with all the other evidence that is presented.

If the aura of a patient is looking better but the physical or emotional symptoms that are being treated persist, then any good practitioner would recognize the need for continued treatment or greater investigation even though there may be some encouragement to be had from the improvements in the subtle energetic field. When perceived accurately and acted upon with caution, positive changes in the aura are encouragement indeed, as most healing occurs at a subtle energetic level first before it has a tangible effect on the physical, emotional or mental state.

X-RAY SPECS

In addition to auric sight, there are other kinds of healing vision that can be developed. Some of us are able to nurture an innate ability to see into physical matter in a way that is a little like a subtle x-ray. For a healer or therapist, this can be a useful way of looking at a patient's body to help us decide where we may best direct our attention. If we can subtly 'see' an area of tension around the base of the spine then we can use our healing or therapeutic abilities appropriately to bring relief or, alternatively, refer the person to another practitioner with the relevant skills required.

For those of us with a natural ability to do this, development of this kind of healing vision will come with practising a range of clairvoyant, auric and healing skills. Indeed it may be useful to train as a hands-on healer or to study some form of massage in order for this ability to develop and to give ourselves regular practice in observing the human body and energetic system. To begin with, you may enjoy taking an x-ray view of your own body and physical needs.

Meditation: Scanning Your Body

- Sit or lie down with your back supported and your body open and relaxed, your arms and legs uncrossed.

- Close your eyes and imagine yourself wearing a pair of spectacles with special x-ray lenses. In your mind's eye build a mental image of your body or, at least, the concept of how your body must currently look. Next, build a mental picture of your auric field, extending out from your physical body in all directions.

- Breathe deeply and mentally scan your body from top to toe. Where is your body tight? Where is it loose? Imagine that you can look deep within your body to see areas that need healing or special attention at this time. What do they look like? Be playful with the images you choose and be aware of feelings, thoughts, inner sounds and subtle sensations that you may receive in addition to, or instead of, visual images.

- Look at or feel your aura with your mind. Where is the energy strong? Where does it look or feel depleted? Is your aura quite expanded or is it sitting tightly against your physical body? Imagine that you have x-ray vision or a sense of where your energy is over-active or depleted. Visualize healing light flooding in to regenerate, disperse energy or re-balance your subtle energetic field.

- Look and listen for physical messages. Do you have any particular physical sensations that draw your attention to specific areas of your body? With your x-ray specs take a closer look at those areas and see what is going on. Imagine that you can look deeply into muscle groups, organs, the circulation and

the skeletal system. Wherever you place your attention healing light will follow to facilitate physical healing or to cleanse
and repair the energetic circuitry of the body. Within the
aura, imagine that this healing light repairs holes, strengthens, brightens, consolidates and, if appropriate, expands or
contracts particular areas.

• When you complete this exercise, imagine yourself taking off
your x-ray spectacles and make sure you take any necessary
steps to see to any physical healing you may need.

DAILY DECLARATIONS FOR HEALING VISION

• I NOW DEVELOP MY HEALING VISION.

• IT IS EASY FOR ME TO SEE WHAT MY BODY NEEDS.

• MY VIEW OF OTHERS IS LOVING, HEALING AND
  CONSTRUCTIVE.

• IT IS SAFE FOR ME TO SEE MORE OF LIFE'S SPLENDOURS.

• MY VISION GROWS BRIGHTER AND CLEARER EVERY DAY.

TAKING CARE OF YOURSELF AS A HEALER

Here are some key points to help you to take care of yourself as
you develop your healing gifts.

1] Do not give healing to other people when you are over-tired,
   over-stressed or sick. You are not going to do any damage to

the recipients – indeed they may still benefit from your attention – but you will not be in a clear enough mental, emotional
or physical space to ensure the quality of healing and you
may draw too heavily on your own reserves of energy at a
time when you will need them for your own self-healing.

2] Make sure that you receive regular healing, therapy, counselling or pampering for yourself. To be a good healer requires
that you expand your ability to receive as well as strengthen
your ability to give.

3] In common with your other psychic or intuitive work, it
is preferable to create a separate space for healing that is
different from your personal meditation or relaxation space.
Certainly, avoid giving healing in your bedroom, unless, of
course, you are giving healing to your partner. Even in this
case you may wish to do your healing elsewhere and keep
your bedroom for rest and play.

4] Find ways to keep yourself grounded. Working with light
may leave you or your client feeling a little 'floaty' or disconnected from normal, day-to-day reality. After healing it helps
to drink lots of water, wash your hands to help break the connection between yourself and your client and to do ordinary,
'down-to-earth' things that help you to feel connected to the
world around you. I like to have a cup of tea, go for a walk,
have a bath, do something creative or involve myself in simple
practical tasks around the home or in the office.

5] It is good to develop a network of other healers for support and
mutual counselling. Working with a good teacher or a healing
development circle may be important when you first start out.

6] Often after healing or psychic work it is good to imagine yourself disconnecting firmly from your clients, releasing them to the power of their own self-healing ability and re-establishing your own separate field of psychic protection. Here is a meditation to help you.

Meditation: Psychic Shields

• Once you have completed healing and have taken care of your client's immediate needs or questions, make a break by being alone for a while and imagining the two of you effectively separating from each other.

• Breathe deeply and relax, picturing your client continuing to heal her- or himself in the appropriate way. Even if you are in an ongoing healing relationship with regular healing sessions scheduled, imagine this person able to take care of her- or himself in the intervening time without your help. In your mind, release your client to the power of her or his own healing resources.

• Next, imagine your client in a cocoon of healing light, safe and protected. See yourself in a cocoon of light too, shielded from most outside influences but magnetic to the love, support and healing you require for your own needs to be met. You are safe in your own bubble of energy. Give that bubble a colour which you instinctively feel would be relaxing, energizing or protective for you at this time. Within your bubble, take some time to rest and relax, acknowledge yourself for the healing you have given and do something ordinary, like having a nice cup of tea!

chapter six

CHANNELLING AND DIVINATION

WHAT IS CHANNELLING?

Channelling is a term that encompasses a variety of psychic skills. A channel is someone who acts as a vehicle for information or energy that originates from sources beyond our regular, conscious awareness. Numerous psychics practise direct verbal channelling, the channelling of psychic art or automatic writing. They may be channelling wisdom from their own higher consciousness or, alternatively, their higher mind may act as a bridge for information from their guides or the guides of their clients. As I have mentioned before, channelling in its widest sense also includes the channelling of healing light, all psychic work and all aspects of the creative process, but in this chapter I will concentrate upon the direct channelling of verbal, written and visual information.

Many people place great store by channelled information, imagining that if guidance is channelled then it is automatically going to be more wise and more appropriate than guidance that is received directly from friends, family members or colleagues. This is not always the case. As with all psychic work it is important to be selective, as the quality of information will vary from channel to channel and from guide to guide. However, good channelling can give us a greater perspective on our lives and spiritual development. The wisdom provided may be less cluttered by human moods and dramas than some of the other advice we may receive.

DIRECT VERBAL CHANNELLING

The skills of direct verbal channelling are often exactly the same as abilities which have been traditionally described as mediumship. Channels or mediums allow their own personality to temporarily step aside so that the personality of a spirit guide can speak directly through them. Some channels or mediums who operate in this way devote their lives to working with one specific guide, building up a strong link that allows for a breadth of information over a long period of time. A guide and a channel will often choose each other because they have a similar spiritual purpose or because they were connected to each other before, perhaps in a previous life.

Other channels I have known work with a number of spirit guides. Channelling more than one guide can bring a greater variety of valuable information but may preclude the depth and detail of a one-to-one relationship. As with physical relationships, some of us like to develop regular, ongoing working partnerships while others prefer to move around more. One approach is not necessarily better than another, they are just different. Some channels seem to work with a collective intelligence or a specific group of guides who may nominate one or two personalities to speak for them, while others may just have one guide who can act as a bridge for information from other sources. The dynamic involved usually reflects the nature of the information channelled and the specific skills of all parties.

Direct verbal channelling entails the use of trance states. The channel relaxes into some degree of trance so that her or his own personality does not get in the way of the information to be transmitted. Many old-style mediums used to work in a state of deep trance, and some still do. A deep trance can be described as going into a state of deep sleep, remaining conscious at some level but being generally unaware of the specific information that is coming through or of the time that is elapsing.

More common than deep trance work, and perhaps more appropriate in recent times, is the practice of assuming a light trance for the purposes of channelling. Some light trance states can be quite similar to deep trance in that the channel may still assume a depth of relaxation or become disconnected from normal waking reality, but a degree of conscious awareness remains. While there is a greater risk of the information becoming distorted by the personality of the channel, this does allow for a healthy balance of inspired guidance and rational thought. I tend to assume a light trance state when I channel, although, even after a light trance sitting, I am sometimes surprised by the nature of the information that is channelled through me. Listening back to recordings of my voice can be like hearing the information for the first time.

To some extent, the personality of the channel remains involved despite the depth of the trance or the strength of the guidance. Perhaps this is a good thing. A certain amount of channelling comes directly from the higher mind of the channel rather than from some outside spiritual influence, and the information transmitted can still be highly valuable for the channel and the recipient alike. What is more, guides often choose their channels because they have a natural human ability to offer valid guidance to the people who seek their help. Whether you are developing as a channel yourself or wishing to consult a channel for inspiration and support, it is important to remember that the information received is to be acted upon with discernment rather than automatically accepted at face value. With this in mind you will probably derive great benefit from channelling sessions.

Many channels appear to undergo a profound personality change while in trance. Their faces take on different mannerisms and the tone, pace and content of their speech may alter dramatically. From an observer's perspective it may be quite obvious that the personality of a spirit guide may be present. However, there are also many genuine channels who can connect to their guides with minimal alteration to their own voice and facial expression. A sensitive and intuitive observer may still perceive the presence of a different personality, but the effect may be less dramatic.

Whatever their style, the process that all channels undergo is essentially the same: they psychically shift into an appropriate state to allow a source of higher guidance to make use of their voice for a short time. To some extent we all do this when we forget ourselves and utter words of wisdom that we did not know we had previously learned. Our higher awareness and our spirit guides are ready to provide us with inspiration at any time. We just need to be available to receive what is on offer. For myself, direct verbal channelling comes with taking time to assume a relaxed state, free from distractions, and verbalizing the first words or concepts that come into my mind. The rest follows naturally. Here are some declarations and exercises to help stimulate your natural channelling ability.

DAILY DECLARATIONS FOR CHANNELLING ABILITY

- I EASILY AND SAFELY AWAKEN MY ABILITY TO CHANNEL.

- I CHANNEL THE HIGHEST GUIDANCE WITH EASE AND CLARITY

- ALL OF MY GUIDES ARE OF A HIGH VIBRATIONAL NATURE.

- I CHANNEL THE INFORMATION THAT I NEED FOR MY HIGHEST JOY.

- IT IS SAFE FOR ME TO RECEIVE GUIDANCE.

Meditation: Opening to Channel
- Sit comfortably with your back properly supported and your body open, your arms and legs uncrossed. Breathe deeply, close your eyes and take a few moments to tune in to the realms of your higher mind (as described in Chapter 4). Imagine yourself gently climbing into the beautiful light, sound and sensation of your higher awareness and visualize a collection of spirit guides waiting for you there. Paint a picture of what these guides might be like. Are they beings of light, sound and feeling or do they have a tangible shape and form?

- In your mind, state your intention to channel the highest guidance available to you, and ask your guides to help prepare you for this activity. Imagine two or three guides approaching you from the group. These are the ones assigned to the initial work involved in attuning you. What do these guides look, sound or feel like? Do any of them have particular names or characteristics by which you will know them? Within your thoughts, ask questions or state requests. Make it clear that you wish to open up to channelling in a way that is safe and in line with your highest good.

- Picture your guides leading you through a golden door into a comfortable chamber beyond. The atmosphere in this place is both energizing and deeply relaxing. Visualize your guides settling you comfortably on a bed or sofa and bathing your body with healing light. Feel the light gently attuning every cell of your body and stimulating the psychic centres of your mind to receive the highest and clearest channelled information.

- After a few minutes of attunement, ask to be introduced to the first guide or guides who will channel through you. These may be the same guides as the ones who have been preparing you for this work, or they may be quite different. Notice any features, sounds or sensations associated with these guides and, once again, ask any questions you choose to and state your needs. Welcome this guide (or guides) into your life and thank them in advance for their care and guidance. Notice any insights you receive before gently imagining yourself being escorted from this room, back through the door, through the realms of your higher awareness and back to the levels of your normal waking consciousness. Take a few moments to adjust to the environment around you and make notes of any insights you have received or details you remember.

Repeat this meditation, at intervals, a few times over before proceeding to the next exercise. You will need pen and paper plus, ideally, one or two tape recorders. Before you begin, prepare a list of relevant questions to ask your guide or guides. Write these

questions down or record them on a tape so that you can replay
them during your session. Remember to leave a space of three or
four minutes between taped questions to allow your guides time
to respond. Here are some suggestions to help you begin. The
channel that these questions make reference to is, of course, you.

'Do you have a name by which your channel may know you?'

'How else may your channel recognize you?'

'Why have you chosen this channel to work with?'

'What special qualities do you bring this channel?

*'What is the nature of the guidance you will be bringing to this
channel?'*

'What is your purpose as a guide?'

*'What other information do you have for your channel right
now?'*

Remember to plan any other questions that seem relevant to
your life, psychic development or spiritual growth at this time.

Exercise: Beginning to Channel

• Once you have prepared your questions, sit comfortably, close
your eyes and follow the steps outlined in the meditation
above. It is a good idea to have a tape recorder set up to record
any guidance that is transmitted and, as previously stated, if
you have pre-recorded questions for your guide, you may
wish to have that tape near you ready to play. Of course, if
you are working with a partner then this person can take
charge of your list of questions, asking each one at a relevant
moment. However, many people find that simply planning
their questions is often enough to elicit a comprehensive
response from their guides.

- When you reach the stage in your meditation that links you with the guide or guides who are preparing themselves to channel through you, imagine yourself settling into a restful state. Make yourself comfortable in the chamber beyond the golden door, allowing a part of your conscious personality to relax here for a while so that your guides can more easily direct their information through your body and your voice.

- Invite your guide or guides to step gently into your body and softly loosen your mouth, ready to speak. Notice the first thoughts that pass through your mind and verbalize them. When you first begin it is important to risk speaking non-sense, making it up or getting it wrong. The first utterings usually serve to clear the mind of superfluous thoughts so that the real channelling can begin. Just continue to speak spontaneously and trust the process. Your guides will continue to stabilize the connection, attune you to the appropriate frequencies and refine the flow of information to be channelled.

- This process may feel a little strange or unnatural to begin with but it will soon become more comfortable for you. Remember to trust your intuition: if a guide doesn't feel right for you, for any reason, ask the guide to leave and be replaced by another of a higher vibration.

- When your connection is a good one, feel your guide's energy and your own safely merging and disconnecting a few times over. Allow the reassurance and peace of your guide to be felt in your body. Imagine the back of your neck and back of your head relaxing and opening to strengthen the connection. You could even visualize your guide giving you higher vibrational information in the form of balls of golden thread dropped into your mind. As these golden threads unravel they transform into words, sounds, pictures, feelings and concepts that are easily verbalized. When the flow of information appears to dry up, pause for a while and start again.

- When your instincts tell you that the process is complete or when you become tired and need a break, ask your guide to disconnect gently and bring yourself slowly back to normal waking consciousness. Remember to bring yourself back from the chamber beyond the golden door and down from the realms of your higher self. Check that you are firmly back into your body by yawning, stretching and opening your eyes to look at the environment around you. Thank your guides for their support and give yourself plenty of time to adjust before engaging in any other form of activity.

- If you are working with a partner, you may wish to take a break before swapping roles. Repeat these sittings on a regular basis, adapting the procedure and the images to suit your needs and personal style. Always give yourself plenty of time to connect and disconnect properly.

AUTOMATIC WRITING

Automatic writing is similar to direct verbal channelling except that it makes use of the hand you write with rather than your voice for channelled guidance. I have seen pieces of writing that give general advice for spiritual development as well as texts that serve to communicate personal information from someone in spirit to a relative or friend who is still physically alive. The other purpose of automatic writing is to give the spirit guides a vehicle through which to produce a piece of creative work. Indeed, great writers have often talked about the inspiration of a creative muse. In some cases, the muse may have been an aspect of the writer's own higher consciousness, in others it may have been the influence of a spirit guide collaborating on the direction of a work in progress.

During automatic writing, channels hold a pen in their hands or sit in front of a computer keyboard and, in a similar manner to verbal channelling, allow their personality to step aside temporarily. Rather than attempting to control the flow of written or typed information, they do their best to allow their hands to operate the pen or the keyboard spontaneously. Their conscious will, if fully engaged, would only wish to control the nature of the information and manipulate the text into a form that would make immediate sense to the rational mind. With the conscious will relaxed, the higher will or the will of spirit guides can direct the flow of information.

Some examples of free-hand automatic writing I have seen appeared to be so loosely controlled at first glance that the individual words and letters were a challenge to identify. However, on closer examination clearer patterns began to emerge and words, phrases or whole sentences started to build a profound picture of the nature of the communication. With practice, early attempts at automatic writing can be superseded by written language that displays a clear purpose or narrative.

A few years ago a family friend shared with me some pieces of automatic writing. Her daughter had died while still a young woman. She had seemed to have a bright future ahead of her, working in the field of child development and education, but her life was brought to an end by an unexpected illness. Some months after the young woman's death, a distant relative approached her mother claiming to have had contact with her daughter. Her evidence was a piece of automatic writing which, in the weeks that followed, was embellished by other pieces of channelled text. Although initially appearing to be random or even chaotic in style, the passages of writing clearly contained messages from the young woman to her mother asserting that she was completely well and happy. She asked that her mother stop worrying about her and she stated that she was continuing to work with children as she had always planned.

Exercise: Channelled Writing

It is probably best to begin practising this psychic skill free-hand, using a pen that is comfortable to hold. Indeed, it is a good idea to surround yourself with plenty of writing paper and pens so that you are not going to run out of either half-way through your sitting. However, if you are naturally more comfortable working at a keyboard, you may choose to start with this or progress to it after a few sittings. Keyboards may partly restrict the free flow of hand movement but, for those who can touch type, the use of both hands may help to access both hemispheres of the brain, the logical left hemisphere and the intuitive right hemisphere, and this can help to access wider channels of creativity than the use of one hand alone.

- Sit comfortably with your body open and relaxed. Breathe deeply and imagine yourself tuning in to your higher awareness and the wisdom of your higher guides as before. Ask for guidance that can easily be expressed through automatic writing and visualize your personality relaxing and stepping to one side. You may imagine a part of yourself reclining on beautiful silken cushions and enjoying the caress of a warm breeze across your face as you listen to the music of your higher mind. Allow your conscious will to relax so that your hands can be free to follow the dictates of the higher guidance available to you.

- When you are ready, allow your hands to move freely across the paper or keyboard, handling your pen or tapping the keys spontaneously. Take some time to do this, pausing whenever you need to rest and then continuing. When you feel that this process is complete, bring your attention back to your normal waking reality and put your pieces of writing safely to one side. After you have had a break, look at the text to see if there are any discernible patterns. Can you make out specific words, phrases or sentences? Do not be too concerned if your first attempts appear to be nothing more than random scribbles or a jumble of disconnected letters. Automatic writing takes practice to establish both a sound connection with the guides concerned and a clear delivery of the information available.

THE PSYCHIC ARTIST

Some channels specialize in co-creating channelled artwork. They allow their hands to be used for the painting, drawing or sculpture of channelled images and forms. I have met psychic artists who work with people by drawing their friends or relatives in spirit or by channelling images of spirit guides onto paper or canvas. To be a good psychic artist it helps to have first learned the technical skills that any competent artist employs. I have seen a great number of channelled images which, while interesting, would have certainly benefited from more technical ability and an understanding of perspective, proportion and depth. However, some psychic artists are actually taught these skills by their guides and perfect them with practice over time.

If you wish to develop as a psychic artist I would advise you to begin by taking regular art lessons and perfecting your drawing or painting abilities over a period of time before you commit yourself to regular sittings. However, there is certainly no harm in experimenting, however inexperienced you consider yourself to be. Young children, free of the judgements, criticism and limited expectations of the adult world, often produce wonderful pictures. They instinctively know how to trust their intuition, relax and enjoy the creative process. In some cases the images they paint or draw are channelled from their higher awareness or directly from their guides. It is only later that we lose touch with our natural ability to do this.

In addition to the artists who create images of guides and people in spirit, there are others who knowingly or unconsciously collaborate on pieces of original artwork. Some psychic artists have claimed contact with great masters who have taught them special skills or, using them as a vehicle, have continued to add new works of art to collections they produced while still alive. As I have no personal contact with anyone who can do this I am undecided as to whether these claims are genuine or not, but it is certainly theoretically possible.

Some psychic art is also sacred art. Many shamanic or healing traditions from around the world have traditionally included the use of sacred art in ceremonies of healing and as a bridge between the physical and non-physical worlds. The Navajo people, who now chiefly reside in the southwestern region of the

United States, have practices of sand painting that have been passed down from generation to generation. Tibetan monks, too, conduct healing ceremonies which involve the creation and destruction of detailed sand paintings.

Exercise: Creating Psychic Art

Choose to work with materials that you feel most comfortable with. If you prefer to draw then make sure that you have plenty of paper, pencils, charcoal, coloured pastels or crayons. If you are more familiar with the use of paint then prepare the appropriate equipment and make sure that you choose a comfortable spot to work in. It is also possible to do this using clay and a range of modelling tools, but I am going to concentrate upon two-dimensional images here.

- Sit comfortably with your body open and relaxed. Breathe deeply and imagine yourself tuning in to your higher awareness and the wisdom of your higher guides as before. Ask for guidance that can easily be expressed through psychic art and visualize your personality relaxing and stepping to one side. When you are in a receptive state to channel, allow yourself to be guided by your instincts and higher impulses. You may wish to close your eyes as you build your connection to your guides, and to open them when you receive a particular impulse to work.

- Allow your hand to move your pencils, paintbrushes (or whatever you are using) across the paper or canvas. You may find that you are drawn to produce figurative work or a range of images or abstract shapes. Trust the process and have a few attempts before you stop to look at what you have produced.

As with automatic writing, what you produce on your first attempts may not appear to be particularly interesting but it is worth persisting over a period of time before you establish whether or not it is valuable for you to continue with this form of psychic work.

- When you complete this exercise, take some time to disconnect from your guidance as before. View your artwork as objectively as possible without rushing to judge or criticize what has been produced.

THE USES OF DIVINATION

The practices of divination play an important part in the development of psychic skills and in the purpose and delivery of channelled information. I tend to shy away from what is often known as 'fortune-telling'. I believe that nothing is absolutely pre-determined and that we are dealing with current trends, personal tendencies and future potentials rather than destined future events. There is a fine line between predicting a future event and placing a collection of ideas in another person's mind that could facilitate the creation of that very event.

The power of self-fulfilling prophecy is greater than many people realize. When we expect something to happen we often create it. While it is important to avoid planting negative expectations in the minds of others, this tendency can also be used constructively. A degree of psychic work can include information that spirit guides wish to pass on to others, precisely to stimulate those individuals to develop their potential in certain areas. With experience, a good psychic learns to use discernment when passing on information and finds ways to support clients to make the best of the opportunities available to them, rather than encouraging them to anticipate future challenges fearfully.

When I use my psychic abilities to work with other people I do my best to remember that I am a human being rather than a divinely realized soul and, as such, I may make mistakes from time to time. My intention is to support people with their healing, spiritual growth and creative development. I endeavour to help others listen to their own higher guidance and I do my best not to pass on information that would rob them of their autonomy. Many of us grow spiritually through the life choices we make. I believe that the job of a good psychic is, in part, to teach people that they have choices and help them to work with those choices as constructively as possible.

I am naturally focused upon the positive opportunities of life rather than the anticipation of disaster, and I would like to think that my work reflects this. If I do see possible challenges ahead for other people I encourage them to harness their resources and make positive choices, rather than leave them with the expectation that disaster is about to strike. I have known people to live with fear and worry because an irresponsible fortune-teller has told them that something terrible is going to happen to them. Fortune-telling of this kind is a million miles away from the joy and exploration of good psychic work and intuitive counselling. No one can be absolutely sure of the future, but we can support people to make the best of their present choices and opportunities so that the future can be as healthy and happy as possible.

THE USE OF DIVINATION TOOLS

Traditionally, many shamans, healers, mystics and medicine people were skilled in the arts of divination. Depending upon their specific cultural origins they would often use divination tools such as bones, runes, tarot cards, the I Ching or astrological charts to assist those who sought their advice or counsel. Whatever methodology was employed, practices of this kind would allow the shaman to combine her or his natural counselling, healing and psychic abilities in the service of others.

Today many good astrologers, diviners and card readers are also skilled psychics who use their craft as a focus for their visionary or intuitive abilities. The process of laying a spread of tarot cards, for instance, gives a card reader a certain amount of basic information about a client's current emotional, mental and spiritual state. This information provides a reader with a framework that can be built upon using their unique psychic and intuitive awareness. The present and future trends that may be indicated to anyone with a good working knowledge of the cards can be used as the basis for a degree of predictiven psychic reading that can help others to make positive and constructive choices about their lives.

Tarot and other divination systems have the additional advantage of providing both the reader and the client with a strong visual or sensual component that speaks directly to the subconscious mind in ways that are more powerful and perhaps more direct than words alone. This helps everyone involved to externalize thoughts, feelings, needs, desires and aspects of intuitive awareness which might otherwise remain suppressed or untapped. Most sets of tarot cards bear images that represent powerful human and spiritual archetypes; rune stones are tactile

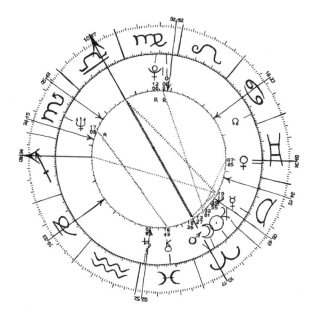

as well as bearing a small degree of visual information; the chart wheel employed by Western astrologers serves both as a valuable technical guide to interpretation and as a 'mandala' or visual focus for the intuition.

I have worked with tarot cards and astrology for a number of years, as well as with many other systems of divination including my own Egyptian stone tablet set, *The Eye of Horus – An Oracle of Ancient Egypt*. True astrology, as opposed to the fun astrology to be found in magazines and newspapers, is a detailed art that requires continual study over a period of many years; as with most systems of divination, when used sensitively it stimulates a deepening awareness of the human psyche and spiritual potential. Utilized positively and with an intention to empower others, divination tools can provide us with an excellent focus for our counselling skills and psychic abilities.

DIVINATION AS AN AID TO
PSYCHIC DEVELOPMENT

The use of divination tools in itself can stimulate psychic and intuitive development. As an ongoing exercise, choose one or two systems of divination to work with over a period of time. While you are learning, you may initially choose to consult the cards, stone tablets or astrological charts purely for your own guidance; after a short time you will probably find that many friends or family members will also take an interest in what you are doing and ask you to read for them.

When you begin to read for others it is fine to let them know that you are just learning and ask for their help and support as you begin to practise. After a while you will probably find that your psychic abilities automatically fill the spaces between the pieces of textbook information that you have learned, allowing your readings to become more rounded and mature. Remember to be as positive, constructive and helpful as possible and, as always, trust your intuition.

CONTINUING THE PSYCHIC TRADITION

There are many unwritten histories of people throughout the ages who have had a degree of developed psychic ability and who have used this ability to serve the higher good of others as well as to help direct the course of their own lives as effectively as possible. Psychics and healers have been given many different names within many different cultural traditions, from high priest and priestess to visionary, seer, medicine man, medicine woman, diviner, oracle, witch and shaman.

As you embark upon the next stage of your psychic development it is good to know that we live in a time when many cultures are once again learning to value natural intuitive abilities and healing skills. Indeed, psychics and healers are beginning to work hand in hand with medical doctors, therapists, scientists, spiritual ministers and the business community to facilitate many benefits for all concerned. I am confident that if you handle your unique psychic potential with love and positive intentions then your abilities will blossom. Your psychic potential will stimulate your spiritual growth and have a positive knock-on effect on all areas of your life and relationships.

The following meditation and declarations are intended to help you strengthen your connection to your higher purpose.

Meditation: Connecting to Your Higher Purpose

Before going to sleep and first thing when you wake up, imagine yourself being bathed in the light of your higher purpose. Within your imagination give this light a beautiful colour, sound and fragrance appropriate for your well-being and spiritual development at this time. Visualize the light of your higher purpose washing through you every moment of the day and night. Picture it, in advance, touching everyone you will have contact with during the day ahead, generating feelings of love and ease within all of your relationships. See the light opening up and creating wonderful opportunities for you, illuminating your pathway to future happiness and success.

Repeat this meditation on a regular basis, always holding an intention that you are connecting to the highest guidance available to you for your own greatest good and the greatest good of all concerned.

DAILY DECLARATIONS FOR SPIRITUAL MASTERY

- I AM MY OWN HEALER, SPIRITUAL TEACHER AND GUIDE.

- I AM A SPIRITUAL BEING ON A HUMAN PATH.

- MY LIFE IS ALWAYS GUIDED AND INSPIRED.

- MY PSYCHIC ABILITIES ALWAYS STIMULATE MY SPIRITUAL GROWTH.

- MY LIFE IS FILLED WITH LOVE AND PURPOSE.

INDEX

INDEX OF EXERCISES

INDEX OF MEDITATIONS